Secrets of The Dark Arts

Psychological Manipulation:

Analyzing People, Situations and How to Influence Others Through Covert Persuasion

Written by

Arthur Cannon

Table of Contents

Introduction

Welcome to and thank you for choosing the **Secrets of The Dark Arts series' Psychological Manipulation: Analyzing People, Situations and How to Influence Others Through Covert Persuasion** written by Arthur Cannon. The primary aim of this book is to provide information, tactics, and strategies that can be used today in order to strengthen personal influence and charisma. This is achieved by analysing the actions, words, and the unconscious non-verbal communications of others and tailoring our message and communicative style in a way that best compliments the achieving of our goals. Throughout the book are techniques that will allow you to better understand yourself, as knowing yourself inevitably enables you to better understand and therefore persuade others. Ultimately, when we are able to fully understand others, their thoughts, emotional states, and personal motivators, our powers of influence, manipulation, and our personal impact will be magnified many times over.

Throughout history, the success of the most learned and wise individuals as well as their overall brilliance has been largely associated with the masterful use of logic, experience, intuition, and the overcoming of current diversities and/or future events. In recent years, science has confirmed many age-old beliefs and has also re-paved the way for a new wave of discoveries. Now, today, thousands of professional individuals the world over are attending seminars and classes, as well as devouring books at alarming rates in order to attain a psychological edge through learning precise techniques and advanced communication skills. Communication has been central to human life for as long as can possibly be imagined and in our modern age, it is as true now as ever it was, if not more so. Lawyers, police officers, government workers, office management, sales execs, TV show producers, advertisers (especially advertisers) and even AI are trained in psychological methods which sometimes err on the side of coercion and manipulation. Most of us are blissfully unaware of the influences that surround us and their attempts to guide and direct our decisions on a day by day basis. But, many of us want to level the playing field and learn the skills necessary to recognise, negate, redirect or create influence and patterns that serve our own priorities and protect us from unhelpful or negative outside influences.

Moral questions often arise for those seriously studying the subtle arts of communication and manipulation, however, studying the methods and patterns involved in such things, even if only for our own benefit is not a bad thing. Skills learned through experience aided by tried and tested techniques which we can develop over time can, in the long term, only help us to grow as individuals. Within this book, we will delve further into some of the moral implications of manipulation and coercion as well as how to overcome them for the betterment of ourselves, our families and our workmates. Developing our awareness and controlling our own reactions are key trends that can be found throughout the book, making striving for better knowledge of oneself, our reactions, and intentions, a pivotal theme throughout.

Establishing a solid collection of communication skills requires patience, self-control, and higher than average levels of self-awareness but the rewards are limitless and affect every aspect of our lives and the lives of those around us. This book does contain techniques that will take practice and experience to master, although the bulk of the methods and strategies covered can be tried out immediately without risk. The idea isn't to control those around you, it's to enhance the lives of and support those around you whilst getting the best out of it for yourself, without having a negative impact on those you come into contact with.

Awareness is everything, and in this survival of the smartest society in which we now find ourselves living, this is doubly true. So, this book was written for those with acuity and flexibility of mind who also wish to make a greater impact on the world around them. The high-level material throughout this book will help you to understand what both superiors and team members require from a leader and how to manage and guide these expectations towards preferential outcomes every time. The book comprises of models, strategies, and tactics that reach across various topics and subjects that can either be used individually or combined to assert your ideas and direct interactions with any number of different people in any given situation. This book mainly uses examples framed inside professional/working environments but whether you are a football coach, sales person, people manager, social media influencer, financial advisor or entrepreneur this book has information relevant to your day to day personal and business interactions and when used correctly, it will greatly enhance your production and progression within your chosen field.

This book was written to work alongside your own experience and should integrate and compliment new theories with what you already know. The methods discussed will enable you to gain greater influence in your workplace and secure your place within your chosen industry or career path. The book contains a number of decision-making models and exercises that when utilised will streamline delegations and lessen confrontations, allowing you more overall thinking time which will in turn boost capability and confidence in all manner of communication. There are a number of key points discussed which at first may not seem necessarily essential to persuasion and manipulation, however, key foundational skills like leadership, trust, and team building, whether utilised overtly or covertly permeate all levels of communication and cannot be overlooked.

You will learn how to harness your systematic thinking skills in order to achieve clearly defined outcomes. The chapters **Persuasion** and **Quick-Fire Lessons on Manipulation and Persuasion** were designed to, at a glance provide useful guidance by providing simple techniques explaining the most effective ways of asking questions, making requests, negotiating and delegating.

Finally, when writing the book, the decision was made to leave out a lot of the long-winded psychological explanations as to the deeper meanings of why situations and people work and react in the ways that they do and focus more on practical models, techniques, strategies, and ideas that will strengthen your powers of influence and persuasion and can be used immediately and perfected over time. The aim has been to fill the book with as much useful content as possible and to provide new material and fresh ideas for both beginners and the more experienced persuaders alike.

Foundational Skills

Holding sway in social situations whilst simultaneously recognising, adapting to, and leading the actions and behaviours of others in the name of achieving our desired outcome(s) is no easy feat. Accomplishing any of the above-mentioned tasks takes time, dedication, and a lot of practice. This section of the book will focus on bitesize individual skills and ideas that can be worked on individually and then put together over time. As each skill becomes internalised and use becomes unconscious, we begin to use them automatically. The skills covered within this chapter are not limited to professional or social manipulations, they are transferrable skills which will continually prove useful time and time again. Learning to recognise the patterns, cognitive strategies and 'get out' tactics that we ourselves use, ultimately provides us a great deal of information and scope when dealing with the intents and behaviours of other people. As you learn and implement the following skills, you will at first begin to fully master your own perceptions, thoughts, and actions and through the mastery of our own thoughts and actions, we can perceive those of others (as well as much, much more). This provides the opportunity to:

- Better understand everyone you come into contact with.
- Communicate in a way which will be understood.

- Read a room or entire social situation effectively.
- Be a better negotiator.
- Offer solutions in a way which will be listened to.
- Influence the moods of others
- Motivate others to action.
- Guide decisions.
- Lead groups to success.

Leadership, or rather having the personal impact and charisma of a leader is a great place to start in your journey towards scaling the heights of personal power and persuasion as it requires strength of character and a varied skill set which together result in high levels of passion, integrity and ultimately, success. The basic ideas, skills, methods, and techniques that follow include much on listening, body language, choice of words (literary expression or diction) and putting it all together in order to correctly read someone can be refined and built upon for years on end, and honestly, it's a lot of fun. Over time these foundational skills will combine to form completely new ways of thinking that support and complement all levels of communication.

Acuity, Analysis, Modify, Act

Acuity, otherwise known as keenness of thought is described in this book as an enhanced awareness of yourself, your actions, your surroundings and the results you achieve. Acuity and awareness of others are both strikingly powerful skills, which once fully developed will enable you to find out if what you are doing is in line with achieving your goals.

After analysing your own actions and their results, you have logical options to consider. Typically, whoever has the most options (due to their flexibility) will have the greater potential influence in any given situation.

Once you have looked at your results and their effect on current circumstances you may need to adjust your efforts and redirected yourself slightly. Sometimes as we move closer towards our goals, we must modify them in order to better define the specific terms and nuances contained within your desired outcomes and absolute goal. This may require you to learn a new skill or as is commonly the case, just a slight change in perspective. Once you have recognised the results and made the adjustments required to improve them, all that is left is to evaluate the results of these new actions or skills.

Wash, rinse and repeat the above method on a regular basis and you will stay current with your skillset as well as gaining a habit of self-improvement and personal development. As you properly direct and re-direct your actions through the analysis of your results you will find your results to be of a much higher quality.

Each loop of acuity, analysis, modify, and act, increases your overall efficiency, in a circuit that constantly feeds itself information which can then be used to bring you closer to your desired outcome.

The effect of this habitual improvement will drive any team forward through the development of the individual, creating confident and competent team members with an embedded culture of excellence. This is one of the ways in which a leader maintains the enduring respect and influence required to manage large groups of people on a long-term basis.

Be A Leader

Nobody wants a boss looking over their shoulder; however, many people require a leader whether they are willing to admit it or not. Leaders present themselves in many forms, but they all have one thing in common, they cannot exist independently. A leader is created through connection and agreement between individuals in an effort towards group goals. The success of such groups largely relies on the ability and efforts of the elected leader and therefore it is the responsibility of the leader to ensure that they do in fact have the necessary skills for success available to them. Self-control, confidence, and congruence are key here. Without these foundational skills, any attempt to lead and direct the hearts, thoughts, and actions of others is not likely to end well. The most effective and respected leaders have the ability to balance tremendous creative power with humble realism, resulting in an air of integrity and reliability which others are drawn to and trust. These attributes also lead to a higher quality of action that is congruent with individual values and a high level of success.

Leaders are invariably master communicators who effortlessly negotiate and navigate countless situations that affect numerous people both inside and outside of their group. The ability to effectively communicate 'cross-party' is fuelled by higher than average levels of understanding. Developing the skills to effectively read and understand others should be considered essential by anyone who wishes to communicate pretty much anything of worth.

A leader can seemingly effortlessly identify the strengths and motivating factors of their team and using the information, sets measurable objectives that can be used as waypoints on the way to achieving an overall goal. The smaller objectives serve as signpost where the current progress can be evaluated and changes can be made if necessary. This system works just as well on an individual basis as it does for collaborative endeavours.

Accept Reality

Being able to recognise and accept reality may not at first seem like a life skill, however, in reality, it is THE skill that is lacking most in modern society. Most of what we see and hear in this modern age is presented to us in a distorted fashion and this has had a detrimental effect on the way many people view both the world and their place in it. This distortion no matter how small the deviation from reality creates vulnerabilities as we act from our perceived reality and not reality itself.

Individuals who operate under the influence of their emotions and who are unable to accept the reality of a situation are extremely vulnerable to manipulations of every kind and are likely to react in a knee jerk fashion. On the other hand, however, having the ability to disengage from our emotions and preconceptions will allow our logical thinking skills to come into play. It takes constant vigilance on our part not to let our emotions take the wheel and run us off the road but if we manage to catch ourselves before we emotionally engage, and if we are able to critically look at and analyse the reality of our surroundings and act accordingly our success will be assured.

Acting accordingly could mean a great many things, anything from changing the overall direction of a project, confronting an issue head-on or even just sitting back and doing nothing while the situation progresses towards an opportune moment. The key point is to fully accept and recognise the situation and know how it affects the likelihood of your success. Once we are able to recognise the key aspects that influence situations and the patterns proceeding them, successfully predicting and manipulating outcomes becomes much more likely.

Properly recognising and accepting the reality of a situation is achievable by disengaging from our immediate emotional reactions to certain emotional triggers.

The most constant and relentless form of emotional manipulation that blurs the lines of reality is advertising. These master manipulations, put there by marketing agencies to part us from our hard-earned cash can provide us with a wealth of information with regard to how many people believe reality to be, it doesn't matter if this projected image is the reality they actually perceive on a daily basis. Learn from these and internalise this information and remind yourself of it when television shows or advertainments pull at your heartstrings and soon, with a little vigilance you will recognise the vast majority of the emotional triggers that you are bombarded with daily for what they really are. Poorly contrived, haphazardly applied, barely concealed attempts to manipulate us into buying things we don't need to impress people who don't care or to entice us to watch awfully written and overproduced tv shows and movies that nowadays seem to be little more than thinly veiled Trojan horses that are aimed at furthering specific political agendas

What Do You Want?

The sad fact is that most people have no idea what they want. They just have a bunch of preconceptions and childish ideals battling it out in their heads that never get objectively analysed and so go unfulfilled and eventually they build up into emotional blockages and eventually mental illness. When we analyse our own needs and wants, what they mean to us both physically and emotionally we are be able, with pinpoint accuracy, to properly define our wants and desired outcomes so that we can realise them in the most efficient way possible. For example, most of us desire mortgages, which is absolutely insane. A mortgage is a massive, usually lifelong debt, so why would anyone want that? The answer is that no one actually wants the mortgage, they want what the mortgage represents. Or even better, they want what the mortgage company has convinced them what a mortgage represents....security. By appealing to our need to feel secure an entire industry has arisen awash with middlemen and charges galore, that we happily throw money at, for the sense of security it supposedly brings. The reality is people want to feel secure and safe and so they should, but in reality, is going into hundreds of thousands of pounds of debt really going to boost your real-life security or even your feelings of security? For some it does but for many more, it brings feelings of being trapped and tied down for the rest of their lives, however, this reality doesn't reveal itself until buyer's remorse and repayments set in.

Gullibility and Susceptibility

Those susceptible to influence and prone to gullibility have a tendency to be easily convinced or manipulated with next to no evidence. The largest single contributing factor in deducing how susceptible an individual is at any given time is the way in which they are thinking. The way in which we think determines the quality of evidence that we require for us to accept the information as truth. The positivity bias theory dictates that we believe most things, only because we have deep-set internal programming requiring us to believe that people are inherently honest. Other powerful factors include harbouring an emotional connection or pre-existing belief that the new information would seem to support.

The problem with this way of thinking is that if we believe everything at face value then we leave ourselves wide open to manipulations of many kinds. This is because positivity bias does not take into account the ulterior motives and goals of the person relaying the information.

A funny thing about gullibility is that the gullible are often quite intelligent and well aware that they are being manipulated for the purposes of others. This is why flattery works so well and why magicians have had been successfully plying their craft for thousands of years.

The difference between gullibility and susceptibility is that those susceptible to the influence of others do not necessarily believe the narrative that the manipulator is presenting, however, the end result is the same, they take the bait. Why is this? Why, when they know information to the contrary, would anyone go along with what would logically seem like the ramblings of a madman? Let's take a look.

Social Pressures

We've all heard of and experienced peer pressure throughout childhood and for me it was one of those things that I thought would disappear with age. Beep! Wrong again. The social pressures of adulthood are like a raging river to the trickling stream of adolescent peer pressures. The need to do what others would think is right is overwhelmingly strong and so is our need to be liked, so strong in fact that many people will sacrifice all semblance of individuality and free thought for the feeling of fitting in somewhere where they belong. Influential social pressures include:

- The need to be liked.
- To feel included.
- Fear of missing out.
- Everyone else is doing it.
- Insecure in their own decision-making ability.
- They can't think of a better option.

Fellow Manipulators, Tantrums, and Naturals

Most individuals who exhibit manipulative behaviours often do so haphazardly and are regularly unconscious of their actions. This ends up having a detrimental effect on all involved. Natural manipulators commonly use extremely basic methods which generally consist of causing some sort of disruption and mental distortion of the current event by having an emotional outburst, like the tantrum of a child. Other more-subtle individuals may use persuasive emotional exploitation with a little more direction. The usual goal of the experienced manipulator is control, benefits, status, financial, or privileges, all at the expense of their chosen victim. These slightly more experienced manipulators are no more creative than the above-mentioned temper tantrum exhibitor. They may get their way slightly more often, however, they leave an unpleasant taste in the mouths of those they interact with.

Generally, those who manipulate others are viewed as devious and untrustworthy, basically unscrupulous scoundrels who victimise those around them. This is not necessarily the case; however, it is in enough cases to warrant us looking into it here. One of the main causes for concern when dealing with natural manipulators is that they have a tendency to conceal aggressive emotions and violent behaviours, combined with a deep lack of compassion towards others, an impulsive attitude, and they almost always act without apprehension or any comprehension of what the results of their actions may be.

On the upside, natural manipulators are regularly arrogant and selfish, which in turn makes they themselves open to many simple manipulations. With the bait being an offer of greater power or privilege, their insatiable thirst for superiority should be temporarily satiated enough to bend to your will.

There will be times when a natural manipulator will hear the word no, this will generally be accompanied by a highly charged emotional reaction. When an aggressive outburst occurs, allow the manipulator to have their say and have their moment. Once the adrenaline-fuelled outpouring is over, the individual will be aware that they lost control of their better judgement, and higher faculties, and in most cases feel pure embarrassment. This is when we begin our negotiation. Find something out about their stated views that you can use and then compliment and support this opinion as if it will be acted upon in the frame you present, a frame that supports your desired outcome and their values. This method draws others to your cause as you enmesh their stated values and opinions with your plans they become emotionally attached to the outcome and will run to your aid.

Rewards

A reward doesn't have to and shouldn't come in the form of an outright bribe, if nothing else this is a crude method that does not add to your influence or skillset. Any offer of reward should be applied lightly. Subtly mention in a 'throw-away' comment something that you know will appeal to their individual needs and personal motivators and also point out that it is a guaranteed side-effect of following your leadership or assenting to your request and not necessarily something you are personally offering. This will make it irresistible to most. To dispel any lingering doubts simply state that you have personally lowered risk to as low as reasonably possible and have kept costs of all kind to a minimum, ultimately making their conversion to your way of thinking a profitable thing to do with little or no cost or risk. When we think of rewards, money is the first thing that usually springs to mind. Although, cash rewards are almost always unnecessary because rewards are more about the feeling of being rewarded rather than the reward itself. Receiving money is obviously one of the best incentives, especially if our superiors are expecting us to work late, work harder and stay sufficiently motivated but the problem with money is that they will always come back to you for more and this is not ideal. Short of setting up a bonus scheme, rewards as simple as recognition can have a much greater personal value to an individual than the promise of cash. The below examples work wonders in the workplace but are also effective in most social situations.

Certificates of achievement work brilliantly with kids and are surprisingly effective with adults too. Something as simple as a certificate for the employee of the month, perhaps accompanied by an afternoon off or a cup of coffee made for them by their manager. This will allow employees to see the standard that is expected of them and that meeting that standard will be rewarded, motivating them to work harder. Make a big deal of presenting the certificate (which can easily be printed from Excel) and throw in a fair amount of praise.

By surprising friends, family members, and work colleagues with handwritten notes we add a personal touch to the message, especially if the message is one of thanks. This affectionate way of giving praise and reward takes no time, costs nothing, works with everyone, and strengthens our reputation for being grateful and polite. When we show gratitude for small favours it greatly increases the chances of a larger favour being granted in the near future. Consider making small requests that are unnecessary in the lead up to making your real request, this theory works in the same way as the yes ladder.

Acknowledging someone in the presence of others has a particularly powerful effect on the individual being acknowledged, especially in social settings. In the workplace, it cannot be denied that openly praising others in public is an effective influencer and motivator. However, when we do this in a social setting the power of praising someone's actions to a third party is dramatically increased. It is surprisingly rare to have someone sing our praises out in public and when done in a social setting we feel social acceptance to a higher than normal degree. If we are able to create this feeling within a person, they will much more likely to follow our line of thinking as they are invested in us being proved right or succeeding. For example, if we introduce some in the following way:

Have you met my friend Kenny? He's a world-class engineer and creative genius.

Punishments

Many people are keen believers in using punishments as opposed to rewards to moderate and control the behaviour of others. Punishments do not need to be excessive or even harsh, they need only to be able to discourage undesirable behaviours. Administering punishment is not the same as negative reinforcement which aims to usurp and replace unwanted behaviours, however, it is still an effective influencer.

Positive punishment, which may at first sound slightly strange is actually the form of punishment that will be most familiar to most of us. It is the addition of a stimulus, sound, touch, or object that by its very presence or happening drastically lowers the chances of a specific undesirable behaviour occurring again. Things like 'Keep Off the Grass' signs, written warnings, physical barriers and even getting a good old fashioned telling off are all familiar examples of positive punishment.

Negative punishments, for example, removing an object or separating individuals in order to discourage unwanted behaviours. Removing stimulus in this way is a simple and effective way to forcibly control the actions of others.

When using punishments as a method of influencing and manipulating others it is essential that we remember to install a new behaviour or action to replace the old behaviour, one that meets expected requirements, however, ideally it should also serve, in some way the same function as the behaviour that has been replaced. If we are to change or decrease unwanted behaviours without replacing them with more desirable ones, we must use positive reinforcements. Finally, whether we used rewards as mentioned above or punishments as discussed here, the important thing is to remember is that we must be consistent in order to send a clear message that will enact change.

Influencing the Lazy

A lackadaisical attitude in an individual is something we can work with because those who are lazy in their actions are more than likely lazy in both their thought processes and decision-making criteria. In the absence of more compelling motivating factors like danger or financial gain, we will in most case follow the path of least resistance in order to conserve energy. This is not limited to walks in the woods, our brains are also keen to follow the easiest and most familiar neural pathways wherever possible in order to save time. Typically, instead of considering all the details, or even the likelihood of success resulting from taking a particular course action, most people's key considerations are the time and energy that will need to be expended in completing a task. The usual result is an action that is facilitated and supported by the environment in some way. People do not view the environment as information to be consciously and deliberately considered, they simply do what is quickest, easiest, and takes the least energy.

If we want to convert others to our way of thinking we need only frame our way as easy and the 'other' way as difficult, costly, or unnecessary. Make desirable behaviours easy and deliberately make unwanted ones hard or overly complicated. Offer multiple solutions, all of which are overly complicated or drag out the process and then propose your real idea, which is simpler and easier for all to complete and understand. The general consensus will no doubt follow the clear and simple route you propose. A good example is the effect pension scheme opt-outs have had on people's saving habits. Given the choice to opt-in many people will decline to take part in a pension programme. However, when changes were made so that individuals were required to opt-out of the pension scheme the vast majority of employees chose not to do so, resulting in a great deal many more people saving larger amounts towards their future retirement. Something as simple as placing a lesser known brand on a more convenient to reach shelf will dissuade customers from reaching up to a higher shelf for a more well-known brand. Logos and brands gain their power from the same principle, in recognising and choosing a brand we already know we eliminate the brains need to evaluate any new information. We tell ourselves we trust our chosen brand and that the lesser known brand's products are inferior, that's the reason they are lesser known in the first place, but in reality, this is usually not the case. We simply buy the brands we know because of our lackadaisical attitudes.

Another subtle way of influencing the lazy is by offering them a shortcut. Terms like 'cutting out the middle man', 'this will allow us to skip ahead' will help set the tone, however, providing examples of others who have succeeded using the method you propose will add serious weight to your 'message'. If possible, mention discussing the idea with a superior or someone who your audience respects in some way and make them aware that they agreed with your plan of action, this should close the deal. If we make it clear that we have spent time and energy on researching our standpoint and display some sort of measure of the pros and cons this too should be enough to persuade others to follow you.

Critical Thinking Skills

What the gullible lack is logical, critical thinking skills and make no mistake about it, the quality of our lives is primarily determined by the quality of our thoughts and the decisions we make. Our brains sieve through between 30,000 and 40,000 thoughts every day. Many of these decisions are unconscious, however, thousands more are made consciously, which means that we are exposed to thousands of opportunities every day where we can either make choices that improve our lives or mistakes which limit our options and current situation. Critical thinking can be defined as rational reasoning, focussed on defining the most effective course of action. This requires high levels of self-control and creativity as we observe and evaluate, analyse and conceptualise, and reflect on our experiences in order to properly communicate with others, find the truth in matters, and succeed in our actions.

Mastering critical thinking skills allows us to overcome our cognitive biases (more on these later), some of which have effects that, when measured over a lifetime are nothing short of catastrophic. We can define these cognitive biases as irrational thought processes that repeatedly infect the decision-making process, leading us to make decisions that have less than desirable outcomes. Some of the more common examples of cognitive bias are:

- **Anchoring** is an overwhelmingly common form of cognitive bias that occurs when we rely too much on a single piece of information which we then refer back to time and time again in the decision-making process and is more often than not the first piece of information we acquire on the subject that causes us to have an emotional response.
- **The Back-Fire Effect** is a particularly dangerous phenomenon which happens when new information contrary to or even completely disproving our current beliefs actually strengthens our pre-existing beliefs as opposed to the logical result of dispelling them.
- An **Availability Cascade Effect** comes into play when we are exposed to the same information (or disinformation) over and over. We may instantly reject the information as foolish, however, if we see the same information occurring again and again (such as online) eventually it begins to gain credibility.
- **The Self-Support Bias** causes us to believe our decision-making skills are more efficient than they actually are as we have a tendency to ignore many glaring mistakes and to remember even the most trivial of victories.

- **The Cluster Illusion** is the gamblers kryptonite. It only takes a small number of wins in a row to completely fool us into to believing we are on a winning streak and therefore unstoppable. This false representation of random data causes us to see mirages within information sets and phantom patterns that lead us to ignore clear and present facts. We do so regularly as we pursue our agendas but invariably these behaviours either dampen our efforts or stop them dead in the water.
- **Continued Influence** is a psychological phenomenon that occurs when past misinformation, even when disproven still emotionally affects our decision-making process.
- **The Default Theory** dictates that when confronted with a number of different options people will usually opt for the default settings, completely ignoring all other options.

Improving Your Critical Thinking Skills

Without critical thinking skills we blunder from situation to situation blindly, living a reactionary existence based on bias and emotional reactions. Improving your critical thinking skills will enhance not only your reasoning ability and logic but also give a significant boost to your communication skills and creativity as your exchanges become more objective, logical and free of emotion the resulting greater effectiveness and success will empower you and propel you forward. As your capacity for critical thinking increases you will plan more effectively, win arguments with ease, accept criticism with grace, and learn lessons from everyday tasks and interactions that others find unbearably tedious. Below are a few principals and methods that can be used to improve your critical thinking skills:

Self-Criticism-Start with yourself. If you take some time and a little effort to analyse yourself, your motives, motivating factors, intentions, emotional reactions, and pick holes in and question them, your critical thinking skills will increase exponentially as will your self-control as you learn to recognise unwanted behaviours and traits that limit your success and stop them in their tracks. By 'drilling' down into the factors that motivate us to act in a specific situation or scenario we are able to deduce whether our actions are reactionary, based on faulty emotion-based reasoning or if they are grounded in a solid foundation. Whenever we suspect ourselves to be emotionally invested in an outcome, we must begin to question ourselves and our motives before we make a critical error. Self-reflection is more than just a chance to beat ourselves up, as we criticise ourselves and reveal weaknesses, we also unveil strengths and skills we were previously unaware of.

Predictive foresight- The ability to analyse and understand the hows and whys of why we approach certain situations in the way we do leads us to an aptitude for recognising the inner motives and intensions of others. Over time these skills evolve into foresight as we recognise and internalise particular behaviours and reactions of other people, we see patterns and begin to develop a particularly keen sense of predictive foresight. This predictive foresight allows us to consider all the possible outcomes from a particular course of action and is without doubt one of the most useful skills we can develop. Being able to look into the future and effectively see the most likely course of action an individual will take, given particular circumstances, allows us to analyse the impact of a decision before making anyone aware of your position.

Analysis- Our brains absorb incredible amounts of information each and every day, the extent of this never-ending stream can easily overwhelm our limited cognitive resources, diminishing our decision-making abilities and at times even causing us to appear foolish. To combat this our brains are always on the lookout for recognisable patterns, something to which it can assign a preconceived label in an attempt to categorise the situation in a familiar way so that it can be dealt with accordingly. There is a flaw in this theory in that by blanketing circumstances, contexts, and situations with pre-packaged ideals we miss the smaller details and intricacies that time and time again will come back to haunt us. By employing our critical thinking skills, we are able to break down exactly what is happening and what is being said and then separate our own emotions and reactions from the rest of the information. This type of dissection of information allows us to properly understand all arguments, positions, everyone's bottom lines, and what needs to happen. Only after gathering and analysing all such information can we truly make fully informed and objective decisions.

Focussed Listening- It is surprisingly difficult to both listen and think effectively at the same time. However, to be effective critical thinkers we must be able to focus on what someone is saying, instead of simple waiting for our turn to speak. Do not waste time holding back reactive responses until you get a chance to speak, simply absorb their message, digest it, and understand what this person is trying to communicate to you. Doing so will also save you a lot of time and energy as typically, a conversation will go around in endless circles until both parties feel that they have been understood in some way. Focussed listening allows us to deepen our understanding of the other party, their wants and needs but also gives us an opportunity to strengthen rapport, and all in a way that actually saves us time and energy.

Non-Combatant Communication- Society today is infected with many psychological issues stemming from a number of root causes, one of the most commonplace yet useless of these problems is regularly known as zero-sum thinking. Zero-sum thinking developed at some point during the evolution of human 'social' brain and is based on three main motivations:

1. **Resources are scarce, there is not enough to go around.**

2. **I must not share information and knowledge as others will use this against me.**

3. **The misfortune of others helps me. In other words, my success is added to and assured by the failure of others. Hurting others is good for me.**

However, in reality:

1. **The available resources are greater than any individual could ever imagine let alone use.**
2. **Any resources you do not currently possess can either be created or acquired.**
3. **The open sharing of knowledge allows all parties to properly strategize, which leads to collaboration and innovation.**

And so, if ever you catch yourself thinking or behaving as if any of the above are true, replace them with their respective counterpart and realign your thinking with reality. We all recognise combatant communicators, those who feel the need to beat others into submission with their aggressive tone and temperament but if we examine them a little closer we can see that their influence goes no further than the current conversation and that in fact, due to their combative attitude it is very likely that their ideas will not be followed up on, even if they are provisionally accepted by the group. A common cause for this is that many people feel that if someone does not like their idea, it means they in fact do not like them, they take any questioning and criticism as a personal attack and so they protect their viewpoint as if they were protecting themselves, a method that routinely blinds them to the ideas and views of others. The same others who see this behaviour as rude and dismissive. Finally, all depth, meaning. and hope of being properly understood are dashed upon the crushing rocks called ego. Be observant of the emotional reactions of yourself and those around you and pay special attention to any outbursts and meet them with compassion and understanding. Allow everyone to say what they came to say and they will feel understood and at the same time that their input has been at valued, whether or not their ideas are enacted in any way. And this feeling. for most people is plenty, leaving us free to continue as we wish.

The Ethics and Morals of Persuasion

All of us are becoming increasingly sceptical, we are forced to operate as users in systems that are vulnerable, they can be hacked, we can be manipulated, CEOs and Judges bribed, and entire cryptocurrency exchanges can disappear in an instant along with millions of dollars of user's capital. Our emotions are easily exploited hence the rise in the popularity of email phishing scams, pyramid schemes and other get rich quick initiatives. Nowadays, we are exposed to such manipulations so often that over time we have developed internal firewalls to protect us from the less scrupulous members of society. Traditionally, tactics involving persuasion, influence and psychological manipulation fall into one of two categories, white and black hat.

White hat persuasive tactics employ clear and overt choices, for example, Amazon's recently viewed items list, a supermarket prominently displaying items that are on offer, or a restaurant that uses a today's specials menu. Typically, white hat methods are undisguised, simple to understand, and are mutually beneficial in some way. There's nothing at all wrong with using white hat methods to influence people, they are clear, honest, and provide enough information for individuals to be able to make fully informed decisions. In interpersonal situations white hat methods commonly consist of open trade, promises of future payments of some kind for services or goods rendered now, asking for favours, and outright asking someone to do something

Black hat tactics, as you may have guessed are methods that some may consider to more on the dubious side. Hacks, fraudulent phishing scams, Ponzi schemes all fall under black hat tactics. However, it is an unfortunate reality that many of the slightly lighter 'greyish' black hat methods regularly find their way into our everyday lives by way of one-sided loan and finance agreements with hidden fees and charges, cryptocurrency ICOs and tokens, cleverly worded insurance contracts and pyramid schemes surrounding all types of selling from timeshares (yes, they still exist) to nutritional products. During interactions both business and social, black hat style communication is prevalent, people haphazardly attempt to lie and manipulate themselves through most situations. All we can do is forgive them for their actions because most are not consciously aware of what they are doing, this is why lies and deception are typically so easy to spot with little if any practice.

When we look at white and black hat methods of persuasion, we, of course, have to consider what of the grey. The tactics used by many advertisers, seducers, politicians and government officials, desperate salesmen and other somewhat morally lax individuals are, in the vast majority of cases 'technically' legal and so they regularly get away scot-free. However, for our purpose, it is my belief that we must focus more on the overall intent of the persuader when judging any moral implications of psychological manipulation, persuasion, and acts of influence. This leads us to what we will call ethical influence.

Our aim is to raise the level of our communicative skillset by practicing and internalising techniques and strategies designed to allow for the greater understanding of others, their intentions and emotional states in order to ascertain the most effective way of communicating a message to them which bypasses any resistance and therefore has a greater chance of being accepted by our audience. It is important that we do this without causing any sort of loss or harm to others. We do this by respecting them as we read them, which leads to greater understanding which inspires us to find fair and mutually beneficial outcomes for all involved. By fully exploring the viewpoint and motivations of others we are inspired to behave with compassion and fairness, creating well rounded outcomes that are beneficial for all. We don't want to outright force anyone to do anything that is going to leave them hurt or at a loss, instead, we choose to work alongside individuals whose personal goals can be aligned with our own, if only for the time being. This way (if we are creative) we can hold influence by tempting others to act in their own interest which is ultimately the most powerful form of persuasion there is.

Conclusively, psychological manipulation, persuasion, influence, and coercion are all linked by an ambiguous sense of immorality that causes even those who only study the subjects to do so precariously. Coercion, as an example, is widely accepted as meaning being pushed into a situation in which there are few if any options available and none of these options are favourable or even acceptable. We've all had some experience of this, we somehow find ourselves in what seems like a mere predicament only to later figure out that we were actually forced into by an unscrupulous other. Examples like the one mentioned above usually occur with the work environment and a common cause is that we have inadvertently outshined either a peer or superior and aroused their insecurities and they have deemed us worthy of punishment. All the mentioned forms of manipulation come with their own unsettling associations and even deception for the good of the deceived is dubbed dubious at best. However, if we do not exploit the vulnerabilities of others to further our own goals, often it will result in us being exploited, which is an unacceptable sin. We must respect the freedoms of others and artfully negotiate motives and intentions with the aim of creating solutions that in one way or another leave all involved in a better place than when they started.

If we happen to witness or be the victim of someone who is employing manipulative tactics that we disagree with there are a number of ways we can approach the situation. Often the most effective tactic is to do nothing, give them enough rope to hang themselves. If the behavior continues over time it will make itself evident to everyone else, at which point the damage to their reputation will be done and any influence they did possess will have evaporated into the ether. Manipulators hate being exposed, however, doing so brings its own risk and it is best to do so in as covert a way as possible. We must always assume that we do not have all the facts and so the judgement of wrongdoing can in many cases be justified through circumstance. There are unlimited examples of traditional practices that employ some form of deception and more often than not this is welcome and is in all likelihood the reason for the success of the practice. For reasons like this, we must engage in manipulation in all its guises and become a master. The only other option is to consign ourselves to being nothing more than a product of our environment and a tool for other people to use as they see fit.

When it comes down to it, we as individuals will all have moral compasses that operate to varying degrees. We all know the basic difference between right and wrong, how it feels to do both and the after effects of both, but here are a few of my own guidelines for those looking for pointers in overall use.

- The **Intent** that lies behind desire in our case is something that should be properly considered from the inception of any goal, it is the first step of the planning stage. By analysing our own base intent, we can deduce if it is rooted in emotionally distorted reasoning. If your intent turns out to be in line with your hierarchy of personal values (For more on this see Leadership Influential Leadership Skills for Mastering Business Communication, Management Conversations and Team Building by Arthur Cannon) it is an intent that is worth pushing forward with.

- The **Extent** of the infringement is in many cases is the final factor in the decision-making process prior to taking any persuasive action. To what degree does the action affect the autonomy and personal freedoms of the others involved? Will the influence, if acted upon have a detrimental effect on the influenced party's interpersonal relationships or stream of income and to what extent? Will it hinder them in meeting their own obligations, and to what degree? Does the transgression outweigh the goal?

- The **Obligations** incurred when gaining influence can be apparent from the outset or can make themselves known at a later date. This is another reason why it is necessary to always be thinking as many steps ahead as feasibly possible. These obligations can take many forms from time spent later on to generalised favours, financial costs, or worst of all damage to our reputation. In all of these cases, the piper must be paid and he will often appear at inopportune moments, so we must carefully weigh up the costs and benefits of taking on any kind of later obligation. generally, it is better to revise an approach altogether rather than take on any form of obligation or commitment. Rather, aim to devise a strategy that fulfils your goals and leaves others obligated or dependant to you in some way without incurring any personal costs either now or later.

Remember: If you find yourself resorting to blunt bargaining or even overt pressure in order to influence someone's position you have left the true path to both power and influence. Finding the way to victory through artful creation and applying it with subtilty is the evolution of communication and will never fail to provide positive results. Take note, if you're doing everything right, no one will notice you are doing anything at all.

Persuasion

Every conversation contains somewhere hidden within it the subtle art of persuasion. When discussing influence and power over others it always circles back to skill in the arts persuasion. How else are we to measure our absolute influence if not by the quality of the conversions we take part in? Converting others to our way of thinking is, ultimately the goal, whether that be the successful closing of a sale, obtaining that long overdue pay rise, or even just getting the kids to go to bed on time. The art of persuasion is built upon a foundation of proven psychological 'hacks', the use of which has exploded in the past decade and is now being used worldwide to persuade people to do everything from buying a product to leaving reviews, inspiring restaurant recommendations, retweets, and likes and even to convince individuals to give up their personal information for no personal gain whatsoever. Increasing clicks, likes, tweets, #', and creating online trends is big business and big businesses invest big capital in those with the ability to exploit the psychological 'hacks' associated with persuasion.

Properly understanding the underlying reasons behind why people make the choices they make requires that we look not at their final actions and their results, but instead the psychological motivators that played a factor in influencing the original decision. The psychological theories, methods of persuasion, and the theories relating to influence explained in this chapter will highlight for you the most powerful and useful approaches in wide use today. These approaches can be developed to suit your particular style and to achieve any particular goal. Here is a list of theories, techniques, and ideas that upon internalising will come to your aid time after time.

The Certainty Theory

This is a method that works in at least two ways. When we display particular attitudes such as enthusiasm, determination, and positivity with an air certainty it strengthens the message and gives an air of congruence to our message. Be aware that coming on too strong, for example raising your voice too much or too often or using excessive body language may come across an excitable or in some cases aggressive.

The Certainty Theory also proves useful when we wish to weaken the certainty of others towards an idea or convince them to open up to us and express their misgivings about a specific topic. By being the first to put forward an idea that solves a problem (perhaps it is in reference to a problem, which seems unavoidable, however, the obvious solution that everyone is thinking is not to your liking), and then expressing uncertainty about it, other people will sense the uncertainty and question the idea for themselves. This will open the discussion up to new solutions, ones that better suit your preferred outcome.

The Minority Conversion Factor

Contrary to popular belief, being the minority in a group can have a disproportionate effect on the decisions of those within the majority of the group. Most majorities include people who are there because it was the easiest option or because the person next to them did it first, or perhaps they couldn't think of anything better themselves. These people are susceptible to minority conversion, convince them with your confidence, logic, and skills of persuasion and you will soon find the majority following your ideas. If the minority voice is congruent and confident, The Minority Conversion Factor has been proved to be an effective influencer.

Priming

Priming works alongside the theory that our unconscious memory faculties are centred around and based upon perceptual identification, symbols, and mental associations with words, items and even people. The theory is that our memories are subconsciously activated by specific associations. These mental representations then cause us to act in particular ways, congruent with the internal cue. The idea is that if an individual sees the colour orange their brain will then reacted quicker when recognising either the word or the Orange fruit. The reasoning behind this is that the word, colour, and the fruit Orange are all closely connected in the memory. This advanced technique can take a lifetime to master and so in order to pay priming its proper dues the **Secrets of The Dark Arts** series has dedicated an entire book to the subject that will be released during 2019. Priming can have profound effects on the memory and therefore the decisions and actions of those who have been successfully 'primed'. Priming works best when the 'cue' (the colour orange in the above example) is introduced on numerous occasions. The more it is repeated the more ingrained it becomes. This is the main reason why advertisements are so relentlessly repetitive.

Everything that we see and hear has the potential to influence our thoughts and therefore our preceding actions. The level of influence is in most cases is so subtle as to be imperceptible, yet the effects are undeniable. Something as simple as a passing glimpse of the yellow arches makes most of us want a burger. An image of a large amount of cash will cause us to behave in more politically conservative ways, we become slightly greedier, some might say. A back-handed comment, for example, a comment disguised as a compliment that in reality draws attention to the receiver's self-perceived weaknesses such as financial, social or racial stereotyping can greatly diminish that person's presence, effectiveness, and productivity in the immediate future.

In conversation, we constantly use 'primed' language as well as 'priming' bodily cues in order to quickly express ideas and contextual cues. For example, we are primed to recognise ambiguous language alongside a sly wink to mean that some sort of game, feign, or deception is afoot and we are to play along for the time being.

Social Reciprocal Normalcies

This complicated sounding theory states that people are more likely to perform a task if it in some way adheres to social expectations of normalcy and therefore less likely to if the task in some way neutral or counter to the commonly accepted social norms. Performing unwanted and unrequired favours for someone will greatly enhance your ability to influence their immediate decisions and actions as an act of reciprocal social norms. If the requested favour or given task can in some way be framed around expected norms and/or social virtues then it is all the more likely to be both excepted and completed happily. Portraying an idea as against social norms is a great way to discredit particular courses of action, even if the links between the social norm and proposed action are tenuous at best, this can regularly be enough to cause a change in direction, preferably a direction of our choosing.

Social Leveraging

However much we hate to admit it, we are all at times influenced by social pressures and the 'need' to be liked. The weight of the influence depends greatly on how we view our relationship with the group or influencer. If we view those doing the influencing as high-value individuals then the level of influence will be much greater than that of someone we view as equal or subordinate to ourselves. Qualifying behaviours such as boasting cause others to view the boastful person as a lower value individual. This is because boasting is one of the main forms of approval seeking, and those seeking our approval are inevitably either our equals or subordinates. Another common form of social leveraging or social proof is that if something seems popular then others are more likely to do it, buy it, or at the very least go along with it. Social proof plays a large part in retail, especially online. A single testimonial from the correct social media influencer can make millions for big brands much in the same way that written reviews by the customers of Amazon (very much appreciated I might add) play a huge part in the credibility and success of a product, whilst simultaneously adding to the credibility of the company as a whole.

Scarcity Sells

If it's short in supply, then more often than not it's high in demand. This key principle and foundation of many a sales pitch is focused on the principle of fear and loss. The aim of the game is to make someone regret not doing or buying something before they have even had the opportunity to do so. If this tactic takes root then you can be sure that the action, usually a purchase, will be completed at the earliest opportunity. 24-hour discounts, closing down sales, one night only concerts are all perfect examples of employing scarcity to spur on sales. The scarcity sells method can work wonders for our social standing. But how do we make our presence seem scarce if we are in fact psychically present? Wordplay and white lies serve us brilliantly in this situation. Whilst socialising, let your friends/colleagues know that you cannot 'stay out' for long as you have previous arrangements. You do not necessarily have to leave the party at all but adding a sense of scarcity will enhance your social standing. This method is particularly useful when dating.

The Hierarchy of Needs

The three main principles that affect our immediate survival are food water and shelter, which together create feelings of security and provide for us a base from which we can explore the surrounding world.

Leading on from these requirements essential to survival are the psychological and emotional needs that interact and either feed or impede one another. The need to express ourselves, to be understood and accepted, the need to belong to family or group and the creation and upkeep of self-worth and self-esteem are all pivotal factors in our overall wellbeing and greatly affect our potential successes. When we experience the above mentioned psychological and emotional needs, we gain confidence, competence, and self-respect, all of which inspires us to innovate, communicate, and emotionally engage those we come into contact with. If we can get others to associate our suggestions and requests with either the sense of belonging, boosted esteem, or feelings of comfort and security, or better yet all of the above, our ideas are likely to be taken on board.

Persuasive Phrases

- The word if can be an especially useful word when used within a question. It takes the edge off our message making it hard to deny. Terms like "would it be helpful if" and "what if" are neutral and have the ability to remove egos from the debate. The word 'if' doesn't reject what has been said before, it simply opens the table up to further discussion and creates a safe environment in which individuals are free to express their ideas and creativity.

- Directly asking for someone's help is a very powerful tool in getting a job done, especially if we are speaking with subordinates. The phrase "I need your help" creates the potential reversal of powers that work colleagues and children will be unable to resist. In addition, and contrary to popular belief, people genuinely enjoy helping others. The feeling of being undervalued and underappreciated is prevalent in today's world and so it is important that we show proper gratitude and praise to those who have helped us. Not only will this, in turn, be appreciated by the helper, it enhances our influence over them, making them much more likely to help again in the future.

- When we describe something as a 'noble cause', even if the association between the sense of nobility and achieving your particular goal is strenuous at best, it adds an emotional connection to your goal that is (if taken onboard) very similar to that felt by the patriot citizen.

- When making a request if we add an additional "this would be a challenge for most people, that's why I came to you" it indirectly lays the gauntlet at the feet of the individual(s) of whom you are making a request. The bait here is the sense of achievement and superiority that will be obtained by succeeding in the 'challenge'. The request really doesn't have to be challenging at all, just slipping in "this would be a challenge for most people" and then carrying on without missing a beat will be enough to plant the feeling of, 'here is a chance to prove my superiority over others'. This alone is enough to spur most people into action.

The Yes Ladder

If we can get an individual to agree to a small request or to make a small succession then we are much more likely to be successful if we then make a larger request or demand larger successions. The yes ladder is an extremely overused yet influential sales technique that when used subtly can greatly enhance your overall powers of influence. When used haphazardly, it has the exact opposite effect and also instantly dissolves and prior gained rapport. And be aware that this is a technique that most people are able to subconsciously recognise if used crudely. When applied with moderation and subtly this method can quickly convert others to your way of thinking. A great way to utilise this method is to ask someone if they like something. Do you like ice cream? Me to. Do you like movies? Me to. It's as simple as that, however, sometimes we are genuine, sometimes less so.

Winning People Over

- Letting someone speak and letting them know that you have heard and understood them is a mutually beneficial way of winning someone over. If all else fails, refrain from explicitly telling someone that they are wrong.
- Keep it cordial, ensuring the atmosphere stays warm and friendly will soften people's resistance to your ideas.
- Encourage input from others so that you can then let the contributors think that the idea was actually their own, making it extremely unlikely that they will then disagree with it at a later date.

At Work and Professional Situations

Understanding an organisation, its cultures and values, and how they operate and interact within it is similar to understanding the inner workings of a single individual. It is common practice for businesses to promote a written list of values. These virtue signalling buzzwords allow us to see how the company views itself and wishes to be perceived by others. When collaborating with, or under the employment of any given company, the more we can align ourselves and our actions with the companies written values the greater our influence will be when dealing with our superiors. Use the company buzzwords as often as possible whilst remaining subtle and be sure that any actions can be explained away through the use of the company's own written values. This will cover your back to a certain degree, cause managers, bosses and superiors to see you as a dedicated asset who respects the company and ultimately increase your scope for influence in the workplace. When conducting business of any kind, there are two fundamental questions that we all (usually subliminally) ask ourselves:

- How do I feel about the individual/organisation I am dealing with?
- Does this feel like a good deal for me?

If we can answer yes to both of the questions above from the outset, before they arise in the mind of our client or collaborator, we have a good foundation on which we can build our influence to either swing a negation in our favour or gain a strong footing within a collaborative effort. There are many methods available to use that can be tailored to almost any situation. Some strategies work best over the phone, some face to face and others through the use of email and social media, consider them all when designing your approach.

Negotiating, the Basics

Generally speaking, negotiation can be defined as any interaction in which two or more individuals discuss and evaluate factors relating to a particular issue in order to come to an outcome that is satisfactory to all parties involved. Negotiations usually follow pre-set guidelines and rules of conduct that aim to ensure outcomes are both beneficial and fair, without which, all would result in the exploitation of the (perceivably) weaker party. If we are to treat others fairly and simultaneously succeed in our desired goal it is important that we follow our own guidelines during negotiations so that we can quickly evaluate a person's position, any propositions, and spot deceptions as well as being able to immediately identify if the person or company in question are incongruent with our own internal values. Below we will cover some of the more frequently used deceptions that occur during negotiations. But first, here's a few influencing factors that can greatly increase your persuasive abilities at the bargaining table.

Before we begin any type of negotiation, we must be clear with ourselves about exactly what our desired outcome is. There is an **Outcome clarification Process** later in the book to help with this.

- Prior to negotiations, we must predict the desired outcomes, as well as the acceptable outcomes of the person(s) we will be negotiating with. Gather as much personal information about the person and their company as possible. Make a note of the companies' values and find out as much about the personality and motivating factors of their representative as you can.

- When choosing seating arrangements for negotiations do not sit directly opposite to the person you are negotiating with. Instead, position yourself at an angle from your counterpart.
- Frame the negotiation as a discussion which is focussed on solving a shared problem in a mutually beneficial way.
- Be clear about what is most important.
- Discuss ideal outcomes and preferred goals and then the factors that currently impede them as talking about problems can quickly descend into a 'my problems are worse than yours' contest. This will obviate any previously gained rapport and create a rift which will hamper further discussion, resulting in inadequate results for all involved.
- Avoid bold statements and closed questions that may elicit a negative answer or response. Instead, use open questions that can provide us with information we can then use to our advantage.
- Discuss any offers that are made in their entirety so that any assumptions are cleared up and no misinterpretations go unnoticed.

- Before rejecting any offer or proposition, consider first using it as the foundation for your counteroffer, adding to it that which ensures your own success but also keeping as much of the original plan as possible.
- After each offer and counteroffer summarise any key points, changes proposed as well as any negative issues that may be likely to occur if the newly proposed changes are actioned.
- Prior to any final agreement, recap the agreement and ensure that everyone feels comfortable and satisfied with the results of the negotiation, as anyone walking away from the table feeling pressured or lied to is unlikely to hold up their end of the bargain or at the very best, they will be reluctant to do business with us in the future.

Common Deceptions During Negotiations

Negotiations can be likened to everything from all-out war and poker to playing chess and getting an unruly child to go to bed on time. In reality, all of these are correct in one way or another. A great deal of our lives is taken up by negotiating one thing or another and so the examples mentioned below are not limited to the business context which has been used for them. Many, if not all of them could, in fact, be used as general rules to live by. Not all of the deceptions mentioned below will at first seem directly connected with influencing and manipulating others, however, overall negotiating skills are essential to the skilled persuader and so by sharpening our negotiating skills, we strengthen the foundations of our influential skillset.

- Whilst at the negotiating table most individuals will lie about their 'bottom lines' and acceptable alternatives.
- As the saying goes "If it seems too good to be true, it probably is" and its as true now as ever it was. If you are offered and accept something that seems a little too good to be true, or the party you are negotiating with makes huge and unexpected concessions, you could very well get stung by the small details, that at the time may seem inconsequential.
- Hypothetically worded questions are generally a good clue that someone is about to propose a deal that definitely is not in your favour. When

someone starts by saying something along the lines of "If I were to ask you to…." or "would be impossible to…" pay very close attention to what comes next as they are most likely trying to sugar coat something that will be very unpleasant to swallow. To combat this, play slightly stupid and ask for further elaboration and more facts.

- Don't throw good money after bad is certainly a rule to live by. It is common to have to pay a number of upfront costs when getting into a project and it is easy to let these prior investments cloud our judgement later in the game. We simply don't want to lose our initial investments. But this kind of thinking is deadly at the negotiating table as it makes us easy prey to all manner of manipulations as we fall victim to anyone from telemarketers and conmen to credit card suppliers and even our own kids! If things have gone south and there is no logical way to save the project let alone succeeded to an acceptable level, then it is probably best to admit defeat and move on. If we are at the negotiating table, we should be discussing new options and deals and so we should not let past investments cloud our judgement more than absolutely necessary.

- Be careful to only commit to a concession after your counterpart has committed to theirs and never make a concession larger than theirs, even if it seems of little consequence at the time.

That little extra, if kept back can be used in future next time we meet over the negotiating table. Also, giving away too much will arouse suspicion as to our credibility, capability and overall competency. If we, accidentally, of course, make a concession before we are able to persuade our counterpart to do so and they do not reciprocate in kind, the best thing to do is to make the other party aware that this is not the way you do business and close negotiations for that day.

- Beware for last minute add-ons as this is a frustrating technique that infuriates all who encounter it. Seconds before the final handshake and pen hits paper it is not uncommon for someone to ask for a last-minute concession to 'sweeten' the deal on their end. These last-minute bites that your opponent is attempting to make could very well be your profit margin, so don't even think about it, just reject it as in the long run it won't affect the 'bigger' deal previously negotiated. Or, make an equal counter request of your own. Resist using this technique for yourself, it is rather effective but the price you pay in reputation isn't worth it, and it could also tarnish the way the 'other side' feel about and remember the deal as a whole.

- Unwarranted or unactionable threats are sometimes made by the more irrational negotiator. The first thing to consider in these cases is will the threat, if carried have an effect on the overall deal or is it more of an emotional threat? Threats are one of the few tools available to the powerless and are usually due to frustration, not an actual desire to cause problems. Never resort to making threats out of anger as this may cause a reaction that is nuclear when compared to your own. Making threats also allows the savvy negotiator to probe your reactions for a weakened position, which will give them an opportunity to exploit it should they so wish.

- Pay attention to any gaps in the information being presented to you and ask a lot of questions. The small pieces of information that someone leaves out usually speak volumes as to their true motives and values.
- Finally, be very wary of those who we catch attempting to deceive us at the bargaining table. Deceptive behaviour is often a clue as to the overall trustworthiness and integrity we are dealing with.

Integrity and Influence at Work

As individuals of influence, we are aware that much of what others assume as our absolute influence and personal impact are largely measured with regard to our perceived integrity. We spend a lot of time around our work colleagues and so it is important that we honour our commitments and behave in a calm and reliable manner. Integrity, in and of itself is a very desirable trait to develop and this can be achieved through honesty, congruence, and consistency, which for most of us at work simply means turning up and keeping your head down. There will be times when the measure of your integrity will be tested to its limits, however, these moments when looked back on are often moments that define our characters.

Our sphere of influence in the workplace usually starts with our immediate team members and the people we spend most of our working life surrounded by. Having an air of integrity in this environment will always produce solid work and facilitate working relationships based on trust. The importance of having trust in, and being trusted by our teammates cannot be overstated. We need integrity to be an effective part of any team. In the workplace and business world as a whole, continuity over time leads to sustainability and growth, therefore integrity is clearly just as central to success in the professional world. In the workplace, it really does pay to have a pre-conceived plan of action. If we can enter a meeting with an inciteful and cleverly devised business strategy that is clearly aligned with the values of those individuals you are trying to convert as well as the policies of the company in a way that complements its current systems and culture we will be perceived as competent individuals who know their stuff.

Being organised allows us extra breathing room in a crisis, these few extra seconds afforded to us by being prepared gives our brains the time to consider and create options. Those with the most options available to them invariably come out on top.

To establish, build, and maintain a reputation of integrity and reliability and to make use of potential influence in the workplace we must adopt both formal and informal methods and models that are subtle, rational, creative, and that reinforce company values as well as ethical guidelines. We must always promote a high standard along with processes, values, and an overall 'message' that is in line with, and can motivate the workforce as a general collective.

An important thing to remember at work is to not make promises that you may not be able to keep. Taking on tasks that you are unable to deliver either on time or fully will have a detrimental effect on your teammates and will cause irreparable damage to your reputation. The workplace tends to focus more on past mistakes than past or even recent successes and so it is important to think very carefully before taking on any 'extra' projects.

Pride and Positive Behaviour in the Workplace

Pride, when properly leveraged and utilised within the workplace is known as organisational pride or pride of service and is an often overlooked and underrated motivator. There are two primary methods available to managers and employers that will create feelings of pride within the organisation, the first being the overall perception and image of the business as a whole. Employees naturally develop a deep-set attitude of pride in the organisation they work for and their position in it, which over time can prove to be an effective motivator and one that is rather durable during difficulties and times of change. Basically, people who work for companies that have a reputation for integrity, coolness, creativity, competence et cetera, have a tendency to believe this perception also applies to themselves and if it is a positive trait, they will go the extra mile to withhold and protect it. Another way to instill conscious feelings of pride within employees is to annually provide a large event such as a free holiday for top sellers. It has been proven that holding small events such as weekly competitions create regular but short-lived feelings of pride that are directly related to their success within the business, which is ultimately the business' success.

Motivating Factors

As human beings, we all share a great many motivating factors and commonalities. The need for food, shelter, warmth, protection, a semblance of a social life, all these things and more we share in commonality worth every other human being on the planet. There are, however, three motivating factors that come into play more often than any other and these are the desire for money, power/influence, and of course, sex.

- Financial rewards, bribes, backhand deals, and cash equivalents have been popular motivators and incentives since the creation of money. Before this time these types of rewards would have been in the form of goods and services (cash equivalents). Money, to most of us, represents true freedom and so it is arresting in its persuasiveness and coercive in nature. It is the most commonly used exploitative power on the planet and has been effectively used to influence kings and peasants alike since the beginning, none of us are safe. Offering cash money as an incentive is too crude and costly, our hard-won assets have better uses than giving them away. So, instead try using the financial loss as an influencer, if possible, explain how the other sides views and actions will lead to a financial loss in the very near future and how your methods will at worst keep the wolf away from the door and provide us more options for the future. Financial freedom can be translated as personal security, this is interesting because it gives us options beyond just throwing cash around. If we can provide a sense of improved personal security, our audience is almost guaranteed to succumb and convert to our way of thinking.

- Empowerment through increased involvement helps us all. Many of us (myself included) have the problem of wanting to do everything ourselves and we struggle to delegate meaningful tasks to others. However, sharing the responsibility for a project or task with one or more people is actually essential to lasting and sustainable success. Here is a technique that will allow you to convert complainers and those with low moral before they infect the rest of the team with their negativity. Try giving extra responsibility to someone who is less than enthusiastic about the project will significantly improve their moral. They will feel superior to other team members which will invariably suit their personality type and also give them something to focus their energy on, and once they earnestly commit their energy, they always work hard because their own ego will by now be invested in the success of the project.

- You may be wondering exactly what is meant by the desire for sex, for our purposes sex doesn't need to be the act itself. Human interaction, acknowledgement the feeling of being accepted by others is as irresistible to us as they are intoxicating. Receiving admiration and finding an affinity with someone of the opposite sex might be viewed as trivial interactions, however trivial they may be, we all crave the acceptance and closeness to others these interactions bring. Being empathetic, considerate and giving those we communicate with our full attention will create worthwhile connections and mutual understanding that will fill those we operate amidst with feelings of security, relaxation, and trust whilst in your presence.

Beyond money, power, and sex the next motivator in the line of significance is the feeling of being appreciated. Showing appreciation has an immediate and lasting effect. People remember those that show them appreciation and acknowledge their efforts. Sincerely showing appreciation to someone instantly disarms them, alleviates their stress levels, and allows them to feel understood. We are all instinctually drawn to those who recognise and appreciate our achievements, so do more than simply saying thanks, look someone in the eye, pick an aspect of their character or actions and thank them for their help in this regard, doing this will make you come across as more genuine. Shake their hand if appropriate and congratulate them whenever possible.

Try asking someone to do you a small favour, for instance, ask them to bring you a glass of water, show them appreciation in earnest and strike up a conversation about them. Ask them a few open-ended questions, allow them to speak and when the time is right, make your true request and make them aware that you will greatly appreciate their help. This technique hugely increases the likelihood of your request being granted.

The ultimate form of using someone's motivating factors to further your own plans is to appeal to their self-interest. It is a common mistake to remind someone of the good we have done for them in the past, reminding them of their past gratitude and the fact they are obligated to us in some way causes them to feel resentment and even anger. Instead, appeal to their self-interest. Tell them what you can do for them in the future and how supporting your cause will further and strengthen their own. Never speak of the past or demand support, only speak of the mutual gains to be had from forming an alliance. Be lavish, talk up the spoils that victory will bring whatever they may be, let them know you will be there to support their own cause when the time comes and convince them that your success will make them rich.

Body Language Basics

It is no mistake in the saying "the world is a stage and a man will play many parts". Actors alongside many other artists are required to master the art of body language in order to fully arrest our critical thinking and suspend our disbelief so that we, as the audience can fully engage in and enjoy the story. As human beings, when we recognise particular movements, postures and behaviours that we associate (from experience) with particular emotional states or traits we both assume and unconsciously accept that this is the case. We then act accordingly. In face to face communications, body language is the largest influencing factor affecting how our 'message' will be received. Others, at first glance, will assume your entire personality which makes using the correct body language essential for anyone hoping to make a positive, lasting impression.

Up to 85% of any message we transmit is done through non-verbal communication with the remaining 15% being the words that we use. If our body language is incongruent with the words we use, our message will be misunderstood or completely lost. When we master our own body language it makes us more attuned to that of others, which enhances our natural initiative allowing us to deduce many things of interest including:

- When someone is lying to us.
- If Someone is hiding frustration or anger.
- If someone is distressed and in need of assistance.

If we wish to be perceived in a certain way or to portrait a certain message or characteristic in order to reinforce or establish our position or proposed action, we must first be aware of the postures, attitude, and gesticulations generally associated with it. If we get this wrong and our body language does not match our 'message', the incongruence will be noticed by the listener, who will assume that we either don't believe our own message, that we are hiding something, or that we are lying. Mistakes like these seriously limit the scope of our influence. We convey our personality and charisma as well as qualities such as trustworthiness, assertiveness, intelligence, and even attractiveness through the use of eye contact, tone and volume of voice, posture, positioning, speed and style of movement.

Poor body language can be corrected instantly which means an instant increase in our overall influence can be enacted right now. Just by assuming particular postures we will begin to feel the emotions associated with that specific posture and so at times when we, for example, need a confidence boost, by changing our posture to once associated with confidence we will not only appear more confident we will feel it too. This creates a loop that starts with perceived confidence that leads to feelings of confidence and comfort which in turn leads to actual confidence, greater competence, and more decisive action.

If we are to influence others, we must appear confident, competent and likable. All three of these qualities are directly expressed through our demeanor.

When used shrewdly, a movement as slight as a turn of hand at the right time or something as simple as holding a pen throughout a negotiation can be enough to assume dominance over many interactions. The **Secrets of The Dark Arts** series will shortly release **The Dark Arts of Body Language** which will explore in great depth the many influential avenues that mastering body language will make available. Here, we will delve into the body language and posturing of specific emotional states. Once we are able to recognise these non-verbal cues they can be internalised and learnt, practiced, and successfully used today to increase your personal impact, credibility, and influence.

Confidence is arguably the most desirable trait to portrait, and one that we actively search for in others. An air of confidence often displays much more than pure confidence alone. The context of the situation or interaction in which people show confidence will display trustworthiness and competence in a particular skill or area of expertise. No one is confident all of the time, or in all situations and unfortunately, it is often the situations that cause us to feel self-conscious, inadequate or even fearful that require us to show the most confidence. This can be accomplished by assuming the posturing and body language associated with calmness and confidence, and as an added bonus assuming such body language will significantly increase your confidence and help you to relax.

Confident Postures

- To assume a confident stance, keep your legs aligned with your shoulders and keep your head up. Breathe deeply and let your shoulders fall back, don't push them back excessively. Aim to keep your feet around 6 to 8 inches apart.
- When a confident person is seated and listening to another person, they will often lean forward slightly showing interest in, and attention to the speaker. This leads not only to greater understanding but also creates strong feelings of rapport in both parties. When speaking, a confident person will lean back if it is comfortable to do so, keeping their head up and speak slowly and clearly for all to hear and understand. This demonstrates confidence in what they are saying and also in their immediate surroundings and present company.
- Don't hide your hands under the table.
- Incorporate open-handed gestures into your interactions. When in intense or deep conversation 'steepling' the hands lets the other party know that you listening when they speak and also displays calm consideration and confidence when speaking.

Dominance

Correctly recognising aggression and other concealed domineering tendencies in an individual can be tricky at times. It is easy to mistake someone's rudeness as attempts at dominance, however, this is usually not the case. Most rudeness boils down to insecurities, avoidance, misplaced anger, as well as many over inward facing emotional states. In reality, the signs for dominance are quite clear and are usually displayed consistently and/or in clusters. These cues instantly allow us to asses any individual as to their level of dominance towards those present, which will, in turn, provide a wealth of information about everyone in the room, their individual statuses in relation to each other, as well as exposing any social insecurities that someone may or may not suffer from. Here are some common examples of domineering behaviours and traits, many of these traits are considered to be primarily masculine, although in truth such traits are not wholly exclusive to the male population:

- Just as in the animal kingdom, it is common for individuals to puff themselves up and assume postures that make them seem as if they have increased in size when making a display of their perceived dominance. The methods used for this include placing the hands on the hips, standing up straight as can be and sticking out the chest, and standing uncomfortably close to those they are trying to intimidate.

- Those who feel dominant often like to lead the when in a group, they are the first to go through doors but rarely hold them open for the rest of the group. They like to walk ahead of the crowd, however, this can sometimes have the opposite of the desired effect as people are quick to grow frustrated with anyone who hurries them along without good reason.
- Dominant individuals regularly speak first, this has little bearing on their actual skills or level of knowledge, they will simply speak. Let them finish, and then shame them with your superior observations and expertise.
- When someone is trying to intimidate and dominate another person they will often talk with slightly pursed lips, hold eye contact for extended periods, and in all likelihood wear a continuous frown.
- When touching other people, those who make a display of dominance will grip your hand uncomfortably tight during a handshake, something that we've all experienced and hate. They will regularly slap people on the back, lightly barge them with their shoulders, and even 'playfully' punch people in the arm without warning.

Hands

Consciously, most people ignore the subtle hand movements of other people, however, our subconscious treats these small movements very differently. In truth, our hands are the most volatile and spontaneous parts of our bodies and ones which we use to communicate a wide array of messages from greetings and requests, to emphasizing a particular point or as tools used to express any possible degree of emotion. The way in which we use our hands is strongly influenced by the way we talk, our speech patterns, trigger words, and any emotions we are feeling in the moment. Using hand movements that emphasize our words when speaking is called gesticulation and when such movements are congruent with what we are saying we appear honest, congruent, and confident in what we are saying. We are so used to moving our hands naturally that practicing the use of hand movements to influence can take some time but with a little focus and repetition you will be able to add weight to any point you are communicating with a flick of the wrist. We can also learn a lot about other people by watching the way they move their hands. Typically, those who have very distinct and energetic hand movements are likely to be the extroverts within the group and those with fewer and more subtle movements usually lean towards being introverts. So, within minutes of meeting someone, we can easily learn important parts of their internal world simply by paying attention to their hands. If someone's hand movements seem sharp and out of place with what is being said then the chances are that they are trying to deceive someone in some way. Here's a list of common hand gestures and what they mean. Remember to always look for clusters of evidence as a hand movement alone is not enough information to effectively read someone's emotional state or spot attempts at deception.

- When people put their hand(s) to their mouth this often signals that they are holding something back, they want to tell you, so much so that they have to use their hand to keep the words in.
- Erratic movements and gestures that are out of sync with speech and context such as thumping a table half a second before raising one's voice indicate that the angry display is just that, a display and not backed up by real emotion.
- Tensing, pushing fingers together is a sign of suppressed frustration, embarrassment or perhaps pain. People often knowingly use these gestures to ease frustration during uncomfortable interactions and assume that it will not be noticed or deduced that they are either emotionally uncomfortable or trying to disguise irritation or annoyance. If someone else is speaking it is likely that the individual displaying the gesture is feeling some sort of annoyance due to what is being said. If the person speaking is the using these hand movements check for other cues as such gestures are a sure sign of deception.

- Hiding the hands is universally viewed as negative, people without proper knowledge or experience consider it to be a sign of deception, which is a possibility. However, when someone keeps their hands in their pockets for prolonged periods of time or keeps them hidden under the table throughout a meeting, they are most likely experiencing strong feelings of insecurity or struggling to hide their displeasure or doubt. The lesson here is to keep your hands where people can see them, especially during negotiations.

- When it comes to our palms, we should try to always keep our hands in an open, palms up position whenever it is natural to do so, it gives an air of 'openness', honesty and confidence. Displaying our palms is at its core a submissive gesture, one that communicates benevolence and trust. An open hand is one that gives as oppose to a closed hand that attacks. Palms down signifies dominance, causally placing your hand down in the palm down position during a key moment in an interaction is as powerful as it is subtle. Assuming this position subconsciously let's all those present know that you are taking command of the situation. Accompanied by the correct tonality and overall message the palm down position is an immensely influential gesture.

- Avoid pointing at people unless it is absolutely necessary and relevant to do so. The position of the hand when we point (with an index finger), is so close to a fist that the brain of the person being pointed at does not distinguish between the two and so (internally) reacts negatively. It is an aggressive gesture that reminds everyone of being told off by their parents and is universally hated.

Arms

Few people are aware of how much information we telegraph through arm movements as well as how easily they are picked up by others. By paying attention to the positioning of someone's arms we can instantly assess their openness, disagreement, or hostility to an idea or situation, if they are feeling insecure, bored, excited, or superior, all in real time because we very rarely moderate or consciously control our arm movements, yet we move them constantly.

- Folded arms can indicate a number of things so be sure to look for clusters of evidence to support any conclusions such as context, the topic of conversation, and the personality types of those present. Generally, unless we are feeling the cold, folded arms signify our resistance, we are creating a barrier to protect ourselves from something potentially dangerous in some way. It is a gesture that corresponds to feelings of disagreement, anxiety, and distress and trying to both contain them and protect ourselves in the process. Avoid crossing your arms if you can help it unless you are trying to communicate a stern front such as when admonishing a child.

- The one arm or partial arm cross in front of the body is a clear indication of trying to control insecurities and discomfort and can most frequently be seen in social settings during group interactions. This posture creates a physical barrier between the individual and whatever it is that is making them uncomfortable but also acts as a self-comforting gesture to help ease and escalating or pent up anxiety.

- Adopting a posture with our arms behind the back may at first seem as if the pose indicates some sort of deception, however, this is rarely the case as this posturing exposes the vulnerable front of the body. Deception is often accompanied by closed, protective body language or incongruent movements. This posture requires us to note the positioning of both the arms and hands. If the hands are lightly holding each other behind the back, the posture generally signifies confidence. When one of the hands is holding the other in place by the wrist this is a sign that the person is holding back frustrations and is struggling to stay silent on the matter. If we notice someone adopt this posture, we have the option of stepping back and allowing them to calm down and regain proper self-control. Or we can push a little further to see what will happen when they finally speak up.

- Arms raised and folded with the hands locked behind the head or neck is often viewed by others as a sign of rebellion or aloofness and therefore negative but in reality, it is usually a sign of confidence. When we feel calm, confident, and above a situation we relax, lean back in our seats and if we are feeling particularly open, we naturally lift our arms and lock our hands behind their heads. It is as open a posture as someone sitting down can adopt so treat it as such. Although, think twice before adopting this posture yourself as those around you may mistake your calm, confident interior and helpful intentions as mocking and insincere.

- When someone folds their arms and grips them with their hands it is a clear sign that they are experiencing very real anxiety.

Legs and Feet

Just as with the arms and hands we can glean a lot of useful information from the way people move and position their legs and feet. Paying close attention to someone's arms, hands, legs, and feet provides clusters of information which when combined with what someone is saying and the way in which they are saying it will be a reliable gauge to their overall state of mind, current emotions, and intentions regarding the interaction. The direction in which the knees are pointed, how open or closed are their legs, and the positioning of the feet are remarkably reliable indicators of a person's emotional state and level of comfort and areas of interest. Our feet are regularly hidden under tables or being used for walking and so little, if any, regulating of unconscious gestures will occur. Therefore, these gestures are simple to read and can be trusted for example, the tendency to point our feet in the direction of our thoughts or to position our knees as to protect us from uncomfortable topics and people. It is worth remembering that the feet are known as the most honest part of the body, primarily because they react to positive and negative stimulants before our conscious mind can intervene.

- When the feet are turned away from something or someone one it often indicates that the person wishes to leave the room, create some distance between the situation and themselves, or change the subject of discussion.

- Restless legs and bouncing feet need to be analysed alongside other non-verbal cues but luckily, lower body gestures can usually be boiled down to either positive or negative emotions. We may be bouncing our legs out of excitement while sitting in a theatre waiting for a movie to start. Or, we could be bouncing our foot out of boredom and frustration as we wait for an overdue train.

- If during a conversation with someone who's body is facing us, they turn one of their feet away this is a sign that they may want to leave, maybe they are already running late and we are holding them up further (look for further indicators to create a cluster). Are their feet pointing towards the exit?

- When seated and someone's feet turn this way or that take note. The movement of the feet throughout a meeting or negation will provide a glimpse into the person's positive and negative reactions. By combining this information with the order and flow of the interaction you will be able to deduce their intentions, priorities, and motivation.

- Legs crossed with the ankles locked will more often than not mean that the person is experiencing high levels of anxiety or stress which they are struggling to contain.

- Crossed legs don't always mean that trouble is on the horizon. It merely means that the individual is feeling closed off in some way and most probably needs reassurance and understanding to allow them to relax and open up. Be aware that women's choices in sitting crossed legged are very frequently due to their choice of wardrobe, in these cases pay attention to crossed ankles, which is a sign of growing discomfort, frustration, and stress.

Handling objects

The objects that we handle and the way in which we move and position them in reference to our bodies and other people are easy to read cues in terms of telegraphing displeasure, comfort, aggression, and self-consciousness. This is because common objects like mugs and glasses, pens, books and notepads, folded jackets are often used as physical barriers that are either held or placed between ourselves and the source of our discomfort. Objects such as pens and other small bits and bobs like remote controls, cell phones and stationary of all kinds are great for picking up on people's frustrations and/or insecurities. How tightly is the item being gripped? Is it being fiddled with and in what way? Tapping objects on the Table or worksurface can be viewed as low-level frustration on par with boredom, although it can also be a sign that the person in question is, in fact, concentrating, just not on you. If you notice someone is squeezing an object harder than necessary consider this an overt sign of poorly concealed anger and be on the look-out for more aggressive behaviour. In such cases, we have the perfect opportunity to either enrage our mark and force them to behave in a way which will weaken their influence and social standing. Or, we can come to their aid in an attempt to persuade them to our way of thinking. A third option, if we are feeling particularly merciful is, we can back off entirely and allow this lucky person to calm and compose themselves before we follow up with a second approach. Fidgeting with objects in general falls under the category of displacement behaviour, self-comforting gestures that help us to relax and reassure ourselves when we feel things are getting beyond our control and as such, should be analysed and considered alongside other contextual information and bodily cues that together create a 'cluster' from which we can gain further information to further our goals.

Smoking

Very few people actually pay attention to the way in which someone smokes, but factors such as how a cigarette is held, how often do they take a drag, and how long they hold the smoke in for provide us with numerous clues as to the person's attitude, assertiveness, overall emotional state and wellbeing, and even what they do for a living. Here are a few examples:

- Firstly, the time that someone chooses to smoke is an outward representation of an inner stress or anxiety of some kind and trying to reduce and control it. Note the events immediately prior to the person smoking to gain clues to their stress triggers.
- Holding a cigarette at the base of the fingers is a good lead that the person may work in a blue-collar position where their hands regularly get dirty.
- Frequent deep draws and holding the smoke in for prolonged periods of time indicates stress

and that they are currently thinking about it in some way.

- Someone who has a tendency to have few draws and just hold a cigarette whilst it burns away probably uses smoking as a self-assurance mechanism, much in the same way a child keeps a security blanket. They may have deep-seated insecurities.

- Holding a lit cigarette or pen (anything of that nature) during a negation is a very powerful influencer. As we gesticulate with our cigarette in hand it is almost as if we are brandishing a weapon, commanding the attention and respect of those we are talking to.

- If someone seems to be relaxed and enjoying a cigarette, pay attention to how often they flick the ash. If they do so excessively, they may be bored or worried. As always, check for clusters of supporting cues.

The way someone exhales cigarette smoke is also full of useful information such as:

- Exhaling smoke from the corner of the mouth is a sign that the person is feeling the pressure and attempting to control frustrations.

- Exhaling in a deep breath similar to a sigh can indicate tiredness, stress, and even an upcoming emotional outburst.

- Forced or harder than necessary smoke exhalation signifies repressed anger and frustration

Recognising the Emotional States of Others through Body Language

The effect that posture has on our emotional state is truly incredible. Our posture and gesticulations have an overwhelming impact on the way we feel. We assume a 'power stance' posture and we instantly feel more powerful and in control of a situation and as we have seen the same goes for any posturing you adopt. If we focus on the body language of others, we are able to quickly deduce their emotions and personality traits, some of which we can choose to nurture, others to discourage.

Recognising the inner emotional wellbeing of another person will yield a wealth of information. To those with the flexibility to tailor their approach and the skills to adapt and to do so continuously, naturally and with fluidity, an entire spectrum of options will present themselves.

Our telegraphing of signals through body language never stops and so unless it is kept in check, can and will continually provide a wealth of information about our feelings and thoughts to those around us. This chapter will cover many aspects of body language and methods by which we can improve our own body language skills and learn a greater understanding of others.

We are all born with the fantastic gift of intuition, a gift that we then improve continually throughout our lives. And because of this, we can often tell if someone is trying to deceive us in some way and even sense small, and sudden changes in the atmosphere of the room. Often this is enough to avoid small mishaps, unfortunately for us, the most dangerous individuals and liars are often the most adept and hardest to spot. Their language is often spell-like and their stories hypnotic, and products and services are beautifully described and presented. Their appearance is smart as is their diction and this is why successfully reading an individual's body language is so important. Below is a list of bodily cues associated with specific states, and how to spot them. They are the most useful emotional states for us to recognise if we are to influence others. Each of these states acts as a signpost pointing to what we need to do next to either motivate, placate, or redirected the individual in question.

Insecurity

People who are feeling insecure will regularly touch and stroke particular parts of the body in order to relax, these self-placating, comforting gestures are easy to pick up as they often occur in clusters of two or three per minute, especially face and hand touching. Negative feelings stirring within causes individuals to touch their face, hands, neck, hair, arms in a poorly veiled effort to calm their nerves. Crossing, uncrossing the legs and other fidgety gestures such as excessively adjusting clothing and shifting body weight are very good indicators of discomfort, nervousness, and insecurity, and it is probably rising. Even if it feels natural to do so, keeping your hands in your pockets for extended periods of time, even on a cold day, will be looked upon negatively. It is a gesture used by the insecure and/or deceptive and so should be avoided at all times. When someone is speaking pay attention to any small shoulder movements as these indicate that the person is not fully confident in what they are saying and is commonly associated with "I don't know". Signs of insecurity include:

- Shoulders hunched and leaning a little forward.
- Overly quiet speaking voice.
- Avoiding eye contact.
- Hands in pockets.
- Shifting body weight repeatedly.
- Self-comforting gestures like rubbing the neck, touching the face, holding hands.

- Arms folded with hands gripping arms.
- Larger than usual pupils.
- Hand Tremors.
- Licking lips.
- Looking at the ground.
- Hiding hands under the table.
- Slight breathlessness.
- Body not facing the person they are talking to.
- Nail biting.
- When sitting, legs folded back with feet/ankles locked under the chair.
- Making too many unnecessary apologies.
- Avoiding making decisions is a common trait of the insecure.
- Holds items in front of their chest as a 'shield'.

Deception

When someone is caught 'on the spot' and forced to come up with an instant lie, perhaps as a cover story, they will often suddenly find themselves out of breath and display rapid eye movements, alongside faster than usual speech, accompanied by long pauses. Face hiding is another common gesture of the deceptive and is often made unconsciously, much in the same way micro-expressions are. Specific self-comforting gestures are associated with (but not limited to) deception, the most reliable of these are those involving the hands, touching, holding, and placing in the pockets, fiddling with jewellery and playing with hair. Keep an eye out for incongruent gestures and anything that does not match or casts shades of doubt on what is being said. If you suspect that someone is being deceptive try asking them to elaborate and take special note of the amount of useless information they provide and watch their hands. Some people will, without prompting, provide an entire narrative that runs alongside their lie as an attempt to appear credible, however, often this type of rambling story, that is long-winded, sketchy, and contains little solid detail can be picked up on by anyone in the vicinity and is instantly associated with deception. It is true that some people may look to the left when constructing a lie but our eyes move rather quickly and so speech patterns and other non-verbal cues are more reliable than the standard NPL approach. Here are a few tips on spotting lies and deceptive types:

- Answering a question too quickly, almost before the question is finished is a sure sign of deception.
- Slow speech and excessively fast speech are signs that someone may be lying, however, search for clusters to support this as they may just be concentrating, depressed or perhaps excited.
- Beware of stories that contain no clear narrative, punchline or ending as they are likely to be covering more important information.
- Stalling tactics like using ums and errs and showing hesitation are extremely hard to control and usually means that the speaker is feeling uncomfortable.
- Those who are in the process of spinning a web of lies cannot stand silence, they are desperate for some sort of sign of acceptance from the other party and so if a prolonged silence happens, they will be eager to fill the void with anything.
- Liars have a tendency to repeat the same information verbatim a number of times in an attempt to solidify their story.
- Deceptive types love to use diversionary tactics when they start to feel like they are being backed into a corner. One of the most common diversions appears in the form of scattered information and stories that make huge conceptual leaps.

- Liars will often pretend not to hear you properly and ask you to repeat any questions in a bid to stall for time.
- Instead of just saying "no" a liar will often respond to any questioning with terms like "I would never do anything like that", "That's not the way I operate", "obviously, I wouldn't do that", "I don't behave like that".
- Subconsciously, liars feel superior to us when they feel as if we have bought their fibs and can hardly contain their glee. This causes a slight smile in the corner of the mouth, hardly perceptible if we are not paying close attention.
- Deceivers often overindulge in eye contact. Listen very closely to those who use unnatural levels of eye contact. Although, avoiding eye contact altogether is also an indicator deception, so search for clusters.
- Liars often bite their bottom lip in the struggle to not let the truth slip out. If this happens mid-story, it's a sure sign they are hiding something.

Fear

Fear is quite simple to recognise, especially extreme fear. We are hardwired to recognise fear in others at a glance as a survival mechanism. This is an ability that much of the animal kingdom also possess. But in the modern world fear rarely means saving ourselves from becoming something's dinner and so our fear must be controlled, in some way. However, it is inevitable that leaks will occur. Experienced orators speaking to large crowds of people will often display all of the signs of confidence but if you were close enough to check you would notice the iron tight grip that they have on the podium in order to stay their trembling hands. As fear begins to develop and progress within a person, they will begin to have hot and/or cold flushes and take increasingly shallow breaths leading to breathlessness. Mild fears such as social anxieties are often accompanied by increased heart rate, sweaty palms and a choked feeling that makes it difficult to speak clearly. Those who are really struggling to contain and control intense fear may feel 'butterflies' in the stomach which could even result in being physically sick if the situation does not quickly change. Be kind and understanding to those experiencing fear, especially those attempting to confront and control it. Read them closely, support and help them and they will follow you anywhere. Below are some points to look for that will allow you to immediately and correctly recognise all levels of fear in others:

- Wide eyes and larger than usual pupils.
- Short sharp breaths.
- Tightly gripping objects.
- Avoiding direct eye contact.
- Regularly jumping to fight or flight like behaviour.
- Not speaking unless forced.
- Head held facing slightly down.
- Feeling ill.
- Higher pitch voice than usual.
- Fidgeting
- Feet pointed towards the door or away from the interaction in some way.
- Slightly hunched, making themselves appear as small as possible.

Sadness

Those experiencing prolonged feelings of sadness which border on depression have a particular way of moving due to the loss of energy caused by real sadness. This results in slow sluggish movement and posturing, they walk continually dragging their feet, hunch themselves over and look at the floor. How much someone slouches and the extent to which the bends the back is quite a reliable gauge to how depressed they are feeling. Generally speaking, those suffering through sadness will tend to a lot of their spare time staring at the floor with their head positioned slightly forward. If someone is persistently staring at their feet they are in urgent need of attention and it is important to provide this for them. If you are unsure as to the depth of someone's depression, invite them to eat a meal with you and observe how much time they spend staring at their plate as opposed to looking straight ahead and engaging in conversation. Key gestures to look out for are folded arms whilst slightly hunched over, a constant slouch and slower than natural reactions, both emotional and physical. Their behaviour will change as their depression deepens and they will become unreliable, at times despondent, and even rude. Here are a few examples of common body language cues associated with sadness and depression:

- Head tilted down looking at the floor more often than looking straight ahead.

- Folded arms/crossed legs and other closed body language.
- Monotone voice.
- Lacking in energy.
- Delayed responses.
- Slow breathing, sighs and repeated yawning.
- Avoiding social settings/self-isolating behaviour.
- Not eating regularly.

Anger

There are many warning signs for anger, each more obvious and explicit than the last and so it is important that we are able to recognise and influence those who are prone to bouts of anger, and lead them into a direction more of our choosing. Often angry types will suffer from regular, prolonged headaches and migraines as a result of continually suppressing their ill-tempered emotions. As anger rises within someone it is common to see their faces and necks begin to flush, they may begin to shake and may even experience dizziness. Those unable to express their anger will display body language that telegraphs that that want to leave the room like shifting their body weight in the direction of the exit or turning a foot to face the door. As tension grows and they begin to feel really irritable you will notice forehead rubs, particularly around the temples and random tensing of the jaw. Clusters of sarcastic remarks is a sure sign that we better watch our step if we intend to avoid conflict, however, if we wish too, we might choose to further frustrate the individual causing them to have a reaction that they may later regret. Do not be afraid of those who make overt displays of anger, this is exactly what they are, displays nothing more and when pushed most individuals will back down. Avoid those who indulge in both angry outburst and alcohol at all costs. There are many body language cues that let us know that someone is losing their cool, the following list comprises of the most common cues and those that are easiest to spot:

- Prolonged stares (throughout the animal kingdom) represent hostility.
- A loss of sense of humour.
- Twitches of hands and feet can represent negative emotions being triggered.
- Increased cravings, smoking, drinking coffee, snacking, etc.
- Tight lips.
- Tightly gripping objects.
- Clenched jaw
- Tapping fingers, objects.
- Partially closed eyes.
- Audible sighs.
- Raised voice and sharp tone.
- Wrapping one hand around a fist.
- Red face and/or neck.
- Obsessively fiddling with objects.
- Excessive fidgeting.

Agreement

It is essential that we are able to recognise when we are winning over our audience, how else are we to measure our success as influencers and persuaders. The best know sign of attentiveness and agreement is the head nod, however, this is easily faked. The type of head nod you want to see is a slight, unconscious nodding. When people use deliberate head nods to appear agreeable or out of awkwardness they often nod overtly, lifting and lowering the head more than needs be. If you spot this kind of nodding slow down and recalibrate yourself to the mood of your audience before continuing. Using head nods is a great way to encourage someone to continue to speak. If we are unsure of someone's story and we nod at them throughout they will likely elaborate enough so that we will then be able to deduce its credibility. An ever so slightly furrow of the brow (when analysed alongside other cues) lets us know that our audience is paying close attention and really taking in what we are saying, this is often accompanied by almost imperceptibly slight squinting of the eyes. An eye squint without an accompanying head nod will often signify disagreement and even disapproval. People who are absorbed in their attention and open or agreeable to what you're saying they will tend to sit still and lean slightly towards whatever it is that has their undivided attention. They will ignore any minor distractions such as latecomers entering the room and will wait patiently before asking any questions, and the questions asked by them will likely be properly considered, contain understanding, useful incites, and ultimately be a positive contribution to the overall discussion. Those in agreement will regularly reflect or mimic the body language of the person they in agreement with in some way even if the individual is sitting and the speaker is standing before an entire room or concert hall.

- Relaxed shoulders.
- Subtle head nods.
- Learning towards us.
- Head up looking straight at us.
- Slight smile.
- Feet pointing in our direction.
- Slightly dilated pupils
- Relaxed arms and open hands.
- Non-forced eye contact eye contact.
- Sitting still.
- Reflective body posturing.

Confidence

Confidence is essential for all types of interaction from first impressions to those we will probably never meet again to lasting friendships based on trust and reliability. Reading someone's levels of confidence in particular situations and their levels of participation during specialised conversations will allow you to accurately estimate their competence in a particular skill or body of knowledge before requesting their collaboration in your project. Often, people exude confidence without speaking a word. The way they sit, taking up at least their fair share of the space, the way they comfortably look everybody they meet deeply in the eye, and their ability to relax and befriend those around them all show deep-rooted confidence that draws people in. whether sitting or standing, confident individuals will rarely shift positions or fidget, their weight will be distributed evenly and the head will be up and straight as will the neck. Confident people are by no means slow to act but they are unhurried, clearly and concisely speaking with a natural flow that everyone can both hear and understand. A measured and steady pace is the trademark of the confident who are generally, unafraid of either inaction or silence. When we feel confident, we are comfortable exposing our more vulnerable areas by holding our hands behind our backs or raising our hands to the back of our heads as we sit back in our chair. Those who communicate directly can regularly be assumed as confident as it takes a certain amount of confidence to be honest with ourselves about our goals and how we feel, it takes much more to directly and effectively express those expectations and desires to others. Be aware of false confidence and learn to spot those who indulge in bragging about their abilities. It is often these types who are of least use in a crisis as their self-delusions, grandiosity, and naivety have an effect that drains the moral and energy of their unfortunate teammates, family members, and friends. Here are some examples of the types of body language used by the confident, they will:

- Face towards the person they are in conversation with.
- Look you in the eye during greetings and farewells.
- Hands by the sides or placed, open handed on the lap.
- Head held up straight.
- When standing feet will be around shoulder distance apart.
- Measured and applicable emotional responses.
- Steady and congruent speaking rhythm.
- Unhurried gestures.
- Stable breathing.
- Leaning back into their chair.
- Leaning forward to listen and focus.

Using the Body Language of Others to our Advantage

Having the ability to tune into others and in effect read their minds through effectively interpreting their body language and subliminal cues is perhaps one of the most useful skills available to the master manipulator. This often overlooked and undervalued approach is rarely consciously used by most people, yet, to those of us with the attention and flexibility to read and react to bodily cues, it is perhaps the most reliable skills we have.

The way in which people position and move their bodies is a window looking directly into their inner conscious. Pay close attention and people will reveal far more through their body language than they are willing to say with words. All of us are, at all times subconsciously translating and reacting to each other's body language, however, the potential benefits of taking the time to consciously internalise and practice reading others in order gain conscious control of situations and knowledge of others true feelings is massively underrated. A little patience and acuity will reveal a hidden world of communication that is often in stark contrast to the words that people say. If we then communicate directly to the message conveyed by the person's body language instead of just their words, the individual in question will be put at ease, feel understood and we will be in a much better position to influence their future thoughts and/or actions. The core idea is to get inside someone's head by analysing their outward appearance. Practice the following methods one at a time and over time they will become internalised at which point they will begin to come together to form even clearer images of the inner thoughts of others. First of all, we must be sure that we are analysing the information in the correct context. Then, we look for clusters of body language signals that are congruent with both each other and the context of the situation, signs that together create a reliable picture of the emotional state and thought process of the person being read.

Breathing

When we feel strong emotions like fear, depression, and frustration it affects our natural breathing patterns. The effect is so strong that it can stop us breathing altogether in the event of hyperventilation or anxiety attacks. Each emotional state has its place on the breathing pattern spectrum, with tense feelings like fear causing breaths to be short and shallow and pleasant feelings of ease like relief being associated with slow deep breaths. It can at first seem petty to interpret someone's breathing pattern, however, with a little practice, it will soon become second nature. The trick to recognising someone's breathing is to let them talk (which emotional people will do if given the opportunity) and pay close attention to the pauses in their speech. Each one of these pauses represents a breath. Many breathing patterns are similar, for instance, fear and arousal, so it important that we don't jump to conclusions. Below is a list of examples, but it is important to remember that these patterns are to be read alongside other body language cues and the context of the current situation.

Fast paced short breaths:

- Excitement
- Arousal
- Pain
- Surprise
- Fear

- Frustration
- Anger
- Panic

Fast paced deep breaths

- This will in almost always mean that the individual is out of breath due to some sort or anaerobic exercise.
- Panic attack
- Anxiety attack

Broken, shallow breaths or long pauses between breaths

- Trying to listen
- Fear
- Panic
- Pain
- Deep concentration

Slow, deep breaths

- Relaxed
- Concentration
- Comfortable
- Daydreaming

Sighs

- Frustration
- Anger (trying to contain)
- Tired
- Bored

- Out of breath
- Disappointed
- Seeking attention

Once we have full control over our own breathing patterns, we will also have a much better grip on our emotions, which in turn gives us more time to think and react. If we are to influence or manipulate someone's emotional state, mimicking their breathing patterns is one of the best places, if not the best place to start. Success here depends on subtilty, mirroring the other person's breathing pattern but not in the extreme, be covert, take a minute or two to analyse and acclimatise to their emotional state and then gently either increase or decrease your breathing to closely match theirs and continue to keep to their pace for a minute or two. Once you feel confident that you are breathing in unison and feel comfortable, begin to either lift your breathing pace slightly in order to help someone to become more active, alert and excitable or gradually calm and slow your breathing to soothe and relax an upset or emotional individual.

Guilt

We've all had the experience of someone putting us through a 'guilt trip', it is uncomfortable and we'd do almost anything for it to end. Self-inflicted guilt is much more potent, the feelings can last for years and the effects, a lifetime.

Generally speaking, we feel remorse when we think or behave in a way that is against our internal moral compass and the standards which we set for ourselves. No one enjoys the burden of guilt and that awful feeling that comes with letting people down and falling short of their expectations. If we can help alleviate these feelings in others, in most cases, we should. This could be in the form of forgiveness, especially when it comes to forgiving ourselves of our past transgressions.

How to recognise guilt in others

Excessive emotions and avoidance are clear signs that someone is dealing with feelings of guilt. Some of the emotions commonly displayed by those feeling remorseful are:

- Restlessness/Unable to sleep
- Depression
- Shame
- Anxiety
- On-edge/Irritable
- Self-comforting body language

The effects of guilt are not limited to the psychological and emotional. Those suffering from guilt often complain of stomach complaints, headaches, and reportedly even muscle cramps. The above mentioned emotional and psychical fallout alongside the self-inflicted and nagging nature of guilt make it unbearable for some, however, it is also one of the greatest motivators available to us.

How to guide guilt to a positive outcome

The cost of carrying excessive guilt is a high one. Remorse and regret are arguably some the most restrictive and stifling emotions effecting western society today. A little guilt is a good thing, it helps us to keep everything in moderation but too much guilt, unjustified guilt, or relentless self-chastisement will hold you back for your entire life. There are a few ways in which we can deal with guilt, the first being prevention. The second, redemption, and the third, forgiveness. There are other methods and many levels to each of the three ideas mentioned above, however, from a simplified standpoint we must either:

- Control ourselves and behave in a manner that does not restrict our actions but also does not have negative effects on those around us.
- Actively put right any mistakes that we are short-sighted enough to make. Take time out to make sincere, heartfelt apologies to those we have wronged, even if the damage was unintended and/or unexpected.

- Forgive ourselves of any past mistakes that were accidental and not malicious. Discard excessive and unwarranted guilt. Forgive those who have let us down or offended us in the past. You do not have to openly communicate this to anyone, you don't have to give anyone extra chances in your good books, you only need make the decision within yourself to allow for forgiveness.

Ways in which we can use the guilt of others to our advantage:

- Guilt, in the workplace, when properly directed, can actually get a lot done. When setting a task or new project make the effort to ensure everyone involved feels some sort of responsibility towards the endeavour's success.
- Another (commonly used in the workplace) method of inspiring others to action is to compare an individual's success with that of a clearly more successful individual.
- Setting conditions for people in the workplace and clear boundaries for those we spend our personal time with will clearly set out for everyone around you the way in which you expect them to behave. These boundaries will no doubt be regularly broken, however, that is when the opportunities for expanding your influence will likely both present themselves and be required.

- If an individual has wronged us in some way and now seeks atonement, bringing them into the fold and setting them to work on a difficult assignment or asking for a favour of some kind will in most cases get the job done. An old enemy is ideal for this as they will go further and work harder than others in order to prove their loyalty and worth.
- Making others feel needed is probably the fastest and most sure-fire way to be sure they will feel guilty pangs if they even consider letting you down.

A final word on guilt. Beware those who act as martyrs and those that claim everything they do is for your benefit. It is one of the most regularly used forms of control. Through inducing feelings of guilt, the martyr hopes their apparent sacrifice(s) in some way will obligate you to their will. It does not.

Influencing the Lonely

The first thing we need to do with the chronically lonely is to get them to participate. Involving those who feel socially excluded in initiatives and social events and focussing on them while doing so will have a profound effect. Asking lonely types for their help will strike a chord and if you allow yourself to show even a little dependency on them and they will swiftly become fiercely loyal advocates. Those who isolate themselves are often brilliant in nature, of well above average intelligence and are yearning for relationships with those around them. Allow these individuals to feel needed wherever possible as this will feed their deep-set and no doubt cleverly disguised inner feelings of superior and grandiosity that are so common among the less sociable. Loneliness makes us susceptible to many forms of influence and persuasion, flattery, repetition, greed, understanding, appreciation, and openly appealing to our intelligence are extremely effective. The elderly are stereotyped as the loneliest people in society and as so they are targeted by relentless fraudsters offering everything from sound investment advice to clairvoyance services and they have a surprising amount of success because those feeling lonely are usually quick to trust others (even though they may claim otherwise).

Frustration

Those who experience regular bouts of frustration are often easy lead and redirected. In their frustration they are unable to think clearly, their emotions are in control and in such a state if they are offered an easy way out, they are sure to take it with little to no consideration whatsoever. If we notice rising frustration in a rival or any other unredeemable, we can choose to add fuel to the fire in order to tempt them to completely lose control or we can choose to seem to help them by offering a quick solution that is at heart much more to your liking than theirs. It is not uncommon for people to feel overwhelmed and this feeling causes them to invert their attention at a time when they should be focussing outwardly on finding solutions. Be understanding to the underlying emotions powering the frustration. Is the frustration caused by a feeling of powerlessness brought on by the inability to act, or perhaps the frustration arose in the process of learning a new skill? If the latter is the case, well that's a good thing, individuals who get frustrated when faced with the reality of their lack of skill or knowledge in a new field it is often a sign that they are used to being at least competent in their chosen field.

Inadequacy

Inadequacy or the feeling of unworthiness is extremely commonplace in western society. It can infect and corrupt the thoughts and actions of anyone, no matter their financial or social standing. Self-doubt is often dismissed yet, in reality, it seriously drains the energy and creative potential of those that entertain such thinking. The funny thing is people who suffer from feelings of inferiority often bolster themselves with feelings of prestige in vain hopes of disguising their inadequacies from all, including themselves. This combination of a belief in the reality that they are inadequate in some way combined with the disconnect from reality caused by the cushioning behaviour needed to protect their unwarrantedly high self-worth creates a cognitive dissonance that ultimately restricts not only their creative energy but their entire lives. It takes a lot to get through to someone with an inferiority complex-those who are decided and convinced of their own weakness carry within them what is commonly known as an inferiority complex. Those suffering from an inferiority complex often develop an exterior wall, an act that takes up considerable energy but serves to protect them from confronting their internal feelings of weakness and inadequacy. They need to be coaxed out of this shell if we are to deeply influence them. However, when they are indulging themselves in enacting self-protective behaviours it is all done in order to present themselves in the best light possible which makes them extremely susceptible to manipulation and persuasion. We all feel inferior in some way, in some field of knowledge or skill in which we are aware of our shortcomings we naturally feel inferior, but this inferiority is our minds way of telling us what we need to do and in what areas we need to do it. Those who ignore this internal signpost and attempt to bury such feelings and replace them with pure ego do so at their own peril. To influence such individuals, we must simply offer solutions and tasks framed in such a way as to support their ego. Do not ask them to do anything for the good for the group or crowd, this will awaken their inferiority (for these individuals the success of others translates into their failure-they need to feel above the crowd), instead tell them that their task is special, essential even, but don't make it a hard task or they are likely to buckle under the pressure. In many cases just holding out your hand as if waiting for the other person to shake it is enough to sway those with an inferiority complex. Simply put your proposal to them and then go for the handshake, hold your hand out three-quarters of the way and wait for them to move the final quarter to shake hands, instantly follow the handshake with a show of excitement to have them on board and congratulate their excellent choice. Here are a few examples of ways in which we can influence those with feelings of inadequacy, so pretty much everyone:

- Rephrasing terms to sound more important is a great way to influence others to go along with your ideas. Instead of requesting weekly meetings to discuss performance issues ask the person if they will consider becoming part of an executive committee tasked with overlooking performance. Requesting that they leave an out of office message on their company email account while attending these executive committee meetings will make them feel important and they are sure to attend any such meetings happily and on time.

- Those with an inferiority complex will often spend a lot of time on social media in vain attempt to seem important and successful. By finding something that you can publicly thank or congratulate them for on social media you are playing a tune they are desperate to hear and they will feel compelled to agree to your overall line of thinking in order to support, in their own minds the idea of the elite individual that they believe you see them as.

- Exaggerating the accomplishments of, and highly praising an individual with insecurities to other people (knowing that it will get back to them of course) will draw the other person to you as they will see you as someone who is not only on their side but also as someone who understands and appreciates them.

Excitement

Human beings really are an incredibly gullible bunch, and most of them can be convinced of anything as long as we have an emotional connection to it. Overly excited people are not difficult to lead, in some cases, it's like leading a puppy or even a lamb to the slaughter, they are the rubes, marks and patsies of this world. Overly excited or excitable usually goes hand in hand with gullibility and often, lies. Emotional people care not for the words they speak. They do not speak the language of facts, they will only tell you how they feel about facts. Sometimes you may have to listen very carefully to notice, but regularly when people speak of an event, product or person, instead of discussing facts, figures, pros and cons, they will consistently tell you how they currently feel or how the person/item/situation makes them feel. When people are excited or emotionally charged, they become incredulous, they are willing to believe things that are not only unlikely but at times completely illogical, bordering on the ridiculous with next to no evidence. Matching their excitement levels and then slightly raising and carrying them into the topic you wish to discuss will cause the other person's positive emotions to carry them along, most likely affecting their decision. They wish to extend their positive emotions and so agree to your seemingly positive line of thought or plan of action. Feelings of excited infect and dominate the decision-making process, meaning that we need only to frame our proposal within a positive emotional stimulant, such as throwing in an added bonus of some kind to sway them to our way of thinking. The key thing to remember is to stimulate one of the following emotional states, laughter, awe, anger, or feelings of angst. These emotions are easily induced and have a powerful motivating effect on the person experiencing them. When dealing with superiors, many of which themselves have insecurities surrounding their adequacy regarding the position they hold, it is important that we provide them plenty of validation, praise their initiatives as well reasoned and then later use the same words to frame your own and credit them for inspiring your creative process, defer any final decisions to them (we may have to anyway) and thank them for their support as it has led you to feel valued within the company and without which you never would have gained the confidence needed to propose your own ideas. Any superior will be hard pressed to refuse this approach. If we are able to connect our ideas to some sort of overall development and progress for our audience it will stir up a number of emotions from greed to pure excitement which we then deduce from reading their bodily cues and then concentrate on stimulating this emotion, pumping their 'buying' pressure. This approach also has the bonus of including all who hear it, this is primarily due to the fact that progress and development are things we all desire, yet they mean different things to each of as.

Bouts of excitement can last for between 15 and 20 minutes so if someone seems a little too distracted by their current excited state, we can always wait for the adrenaline to burn off and come back to our discussion later on. However, be aware that if someone is in the throes of a bout of excitement, they are much more likely to act immediately on any new proposed course of action.

Quick Fire Lessons on Manipulation and Persuasion

Most people walk around all day with their eyes open yet they see nothing at all. People feel like they're in a hurry and feel they simply do not have the time to properly analyse the never-ending influx of information beamed into their head at any given moment. Because of this, people often categorise things into small groups in the forms of sets of (usually) opposites. For example:

- Interesting or Boring.
- Accept or Reject.
- Good or Evil.
- Right or Wrong.
- Fair or Unfair.
- Truth or Deception.
- Worthless or Worthwhile.
- Restriction or Liberty.
- Gain or Loss.

This habit of separating qualities off into couples of very basic positive or negative natures brings with it instant negative and positive connotations regardless of the context and factual details of any particular presentation or interaction in which the words themselves are used or even associated with. This causes many of us to miss the slight nuances and pivotal factors that exist within the subtler shades of grey as well as opening the door to simple emotional manipulations. When communicating an idea or initiative to others, if we pepper our delivery with words that carry positive associations the easily influenced in the group or those unable to come up with something better will naturally gravitate towards your line of thinking. Such words are also extremely powerful when we wish to skate over specific points. If there are any particular points you feel less than confident on or wish to hide, you can effectively do so (in the short-term) within a maze of positive association and a cleverly worded joke or quote.

Plug Any and All Leaks

What is meant by leakage is the inadvertent telegraphing of our position by 'leaking' key information through body language and other non-verbal cues to those we are negotiating with. We have already covered much of this; however, it is worth recapping some of the more revealing, negative leaks as a reminder that, should we catch ourselves doing any of the following, we must readjust ourselves if we are to have any real influence in the conversation or situation. The following leaks are not the be all and end all and as previously mentioned, always be aware that any 'tells' can only be relied upon when they appear within a cluster of similar tells. For most people, however, just one of these tells is enough to cause assumptions and doubts. For instance, hunched shoulders may not mean that the individual is closed off to you, they may just be feeling the cold, but someone else may instantly view the hunched shouldered individual (incorrectly so) in a negative light. Whether or not the assumption is correct, the person thinking it will behave as if it is so. This is why it is so important to control our body language and other non-verbal communications at all times.

- Shaking or bouncing knee.
- Legs folded with an ankle locked around a chair or table leg.
- Restless leg movements.
- Feet pointing away from the person you are talking to.

- Crossed ankles.
- Excess fidgeting and changes in bodily positioning.
- Shoulders hunched forward.
- Lifted shoulders.
- Uneven shoulders.
- Unrequired readjustments of clothing.
- Clenched fists.
- Sharp movements.
- Touching the face.
- Covering the mouth or eyes.
- A tightening of biting of the lips
- Fidgeting with objects such as pens.
- Excessive phone checking.
- Frequent gulping.
- Excessive blinking.
- Rapid eye movements.
- Slouching.
- Raised mouth.
- Clenched jaw/Gritted teeth.
- Holding breath.

As we already know, we telegraph many, many more non-verbal communications than mentioned here, but the examples listed above are all dead giveaways as to your mental processes and emotional state, even to those with little to no knowledge of body language and a limited ability to read between the lines. These tells can also be instantly corrected if we have the acuity, flexibility, and focus to continually monitor and manage our natural tendencies, emotional triggers, and reactions. Stay vigilant, however, remember that your movements should always be natural, fluid and perhaps most importantly, congruent with your message.

A Word on Favours

Ideally, we should avoid committing to favours and always keep in mind that no good deed goes unpunished. People who make requests of us often come back for more and more and we help them time and again, and in the end, they resent us for it. We should also think twice before openly asking someone for a favour, particularly of superiors. Although, if we really do need the aid of someone else the following strategy will greatly increase your chances of success.

If we need a big favour of someone try first asking them for their advice, pay close attention to what they say and take it on board, act on it if possible and openly discuss the results (which you largely accredit to the advice previously given) with mutual friends/colleagues. They will hear of this and appreciate that you listened to and understood them, your success is now linked to theirs and they will now be willing to do larger things on your behalf in order to uphold the image they believe you to have of them.

Tips and Tricks to Use Today

On a daily basis, we face many people and situations that seem daunting and awkward and as a result, many of us spend most of our lives trying avoiding them. Unfortunately, this causes people to frequently feel powerless through lack of experience and when forced to confront trying situations and individuals, end up at their mercy. However, there are a great number of things we can do when confronted with a fool or the issue of how to properly ask for a pay rise. Within the tips and tactics section of the book are influential phrases for persuading others, lessons on creating tools that will ensure our will is carried out in our absence and quick-fire lessons on topics like silence, comparisons and translating others. The following questions, tactics, and ideas were designed to be simple and quick to both learn and use, you can try them out today.

Getting a Pay Rise

You deserve a pay rise, we all do. All too often people are undervalued and overworked, the problem is that most people just accept this as the status quo. Asking for a pay rise can be a nerve-wracking experience but as with most things, the key is asking the right questions with an air of boldness. The method of requesting an increase in your wage or salary detailed below is very powerful and has an extremely high success rate.

1. Pick your battleground

Don't just blurt out "I need more money!" during a team meeting. Your best bet is going to be to request to speak to your manager in private. Be sure you're asking the right person, not all superiors are able to implement a pay increase, don't waste your time, and go straight to the top.

2. First request

This first request is not designed to be accepted; the first request is more of a set up for the killer question.

QUESTION: "Thank you for your time today, I wanted to speak to you because I have a question, and you have always been very understanding towards me. Do you think you can help me? I need a pay rise............." (and then wait).

3. Most likely reply

Bosses and managers routinely deal with requests for pay increases so this is nothing new to them, if they do not agree to your request it will be denied in one of the following ways:

"We can't afford it".

"Wait until the beginning of the new financial year".

"We'll discuss it during your appraisal".

"I've not got time to discuss it now".

4. Killer Blow

At first glance, the killer blow may seem a little forward, and it is. Your superiors will not be accustomed to this style of questioning and therefore you are likely to receive an honest and positive response. Your bosses and managers are inherently good people and want to be seen as such, the killer blow will put them into a position where they are forced to view themselves in a positive or negative light.

QUESTION: "I've progressed a lot since I first started working here, what do you think I'm worth?"

At this point, your boss/manager may take a second to think but the only realistic option available to them is to confirm your worth and therefore agree to a pay rise, the negotiation of amounts I will leave to you.

The above method is tried and tested which has worked time after time. It may take a little courage to ask for a pay rise but rest assured you will receive a positive outcome.

Do you think you can?

We all need help sometimes and from time to time we may be forced to ask someone to do something that we know they rather wouldn't. Here's the best way to ask.

QUESTION: "Do you think you can….?"

When you word your request in this way the question will in most cases be answered automatically and internally by the other person's ego before you have even finished your request. This does not mean that they will outwardly agree to your request it means only that internally they are already leaning towards a yes. If the person has the ability to do the task and there is no bad air between you, in many cases they will agree to help you in whatever way they can. Another upside to this simple persuasive technique is that is completely invisible to all, there is no risk in making a request in this way. The way you frame your requests does not promise success, however, all else being equal, it will allow you to at least gain the upper hand.

Saying No

Generally speaking, most of us find it almost impossible to say no to someone without being left with feelings of either guilt, anger or a mix of both. There are in fact lots of ways of saying no without actually using the word and below we will cover some of the more subtle and persuasive examples.

How to Make Counter Offers

In future when someone puts forward an idea or plan which is either against your values, you plainly disagree with, or is clearly bound to fail, use the following counteroffer technique. This technique has two parts, the first is to initially seem agreeable and the second, to replace or improve the idea which is summed up in the form of a counter offer. Even if we calmly, honestly and openly say no to someone's offer or idea we risk alienating them, which will, in turn, close them off to your ideas. This is especially true when dealing with superiors. When we agree in principle or at least give off affirmative signals we lower the defenses of the other party, making them susceptible to our counter offer which will either incorporate their idea or if necessary, promote an entire change in direction. For example:

"That's a great idea that would work in most cases, in addition, can I suggest…."

Outcome Comparison

The selfish and the foolish are a burden to us all but the following example is a sure-fire way to get someone off your back. The basis of this idea is the principle of what's good for the team is good for the individual. Improvise an excuse that incorporates within it, and is backed up by some sort of team effort.

"I could do that, it will save time today. Or I could finish this first so we meet our weekly team target".

Ask for Advice

If someone who knows or can plainly see that you are busy asks you to do something by calmly asking "could you help me prioritise my workload?" we instantly make clear that we are too busy unless they want to take some tasks off our hands, which they won't.

Counter Request

A novel way of rebuking unwanted requests is to instantly reply with a counter-request of our own. This drastically changes the dynamic of the interaction as the tables are turned. They must now either walk away empty-handed or fulfil your request in the hopes the favour will be returned. This method works particularly well if we use, as our counter request something that we know the other person does not want to/cannot effectively do as they will quickly shuffle away, and once again you will be left guilt free and in peace.

"That's an idea that would work, but first, could you help me see this errand?"

Loaded Questions

Loaded questions are questions that presuppose answers and are usually asked because they work in the asker's benefit. For example, if somebody seems a bit groggier than usual you might want to ask "good night last night, was it?" Or if, for instance, a child refuses to eat their vegetables we could ask them if they want to grow up big and strong. The answer is of course they do, and so a yes is loaded into the question and in answering it the child is one step closer to being persuaded to eating their greens.

Silence

Silence acts as a vacuum and when used correctly you can use it to influence countless situations. It is similar to the way in which the things that people avert their gaze from, often provided more information than what they are actually looking at. To master the art of silence we must practice self-control. We must get comfortable with staying quiet through uncomfortable silences as this often inspires others to act, either causing them to make mistakes or inspiring them to think creatively. Silence as a tool is often employed by those working in sales who often use silence as a powerful motivator. They do this by first asking a loaded question, one which leaves the prospective client back into a corner by their own words and pressure to buy. The loaded question is immediately followed by a prolonged silence, the awkwardness of this silence pushed the customer to answer, at which point the sale is practically complete.

Silence, matched with the correct body language can speak volumes forcing the asker to subconsciously accept a 'no' before you even say a word. As soon as you are aware that a request is coming (one which you want to decline), lean back and cross your arms and breath out through your nose so that it can be heard by someone paying close attention to you. If you are standing, turn your body slightly away from the person who is asking the question and if possible, feign divided attention. Silence, properly combined with the correct body language voices our opinions and feelings loud and clear.

Words to Start Using Today

As we already know, not all words are created equal. Some have a much greater impact than others. Some words shock whilst some words gently slide through our defences and influences the way we feel. Some make us smile while others can make our skin crawl. Here are some further examples of words to incorporate into your lexicon that will increase the overall impact of your presence and strengthen your absolute influence.

Inciteful, powerful, genius, exceptional, outstanding, energise, success, fast, desire, entrepreneurial, attract, impact, likeable, comfortable, share, appreciate, exciting, resourceful, interesting, compelling, empowering, fantastic, vivid, pragmatic, helpful, advantageous, affluent, supportive, masterful, vigorous, dynamic.

Words and Phrases to Avoid

Lose/loser, but, fail/failure, weird, pointless, useless, boring, a little bit, just, so, bear with me, moving forward, I couldn't, I didn't want to, touching base, I didn't have much time to prepare, can't, won't, strict, rigid, maybe, attempt, try, never, catch up, poor, weak, pointless, stupid.

Sorry

Apologising and saying sorry too often seriously impacts your influence and charisma. However, a sudden show of humility and remorse will often soften the thoughts of even the most judgemental. Use your apology as a display of your (feigned) inferiority to whoever it is you're apologising to. When deceiving others, add in feigned weakness such as either financial or willpower to the list in order to make them feel even more superior. This feeling of superiority you have given them will act as your smokescreen, as someone who believes that you think yourself beneath them will think twice before suspecting you in the future and will also ignore any small moves made against them, allowing you to make what moves you will and steadily build your power base and influence from the shadows.

Always and Never

When we use words like always and never, we take the risk of shutting down and closing off open communication to both yourself and others. Other people will feel as if you are attempting to strongarm negotiations and using such words when communicating internally will set up and enforce limiting beliefs which will eventually spill out as either resentments or anger. Annoying people use the terms always and never.

"I/They always/never do this"-Try to think of a time when you/they did/did not do this.

Create Tools

Creating and developing your own tools is a great way of attaining and maintaining influence over processes or behaviours. We can create models for measuring, assessing and dealing with timekeeping, sales scripts, development programmes, and future orientated reports to help secure our sustainability and productivity. Future orientated reports can be extremely useful tools for predicting the coming month's results. As an example of a future-orientated report we could:

Review the total monthly sales for each product over the last three months. For example, if we sold mobile phones, our past 3 months sales could be January=10 February=8 March= 9

Combine the totals for a chosen product for the three months. Following the above example, this means we have a total of 27 mobile phone sales.

Next, we divide our total sales (in this case 27) by the number of months the sales were taken over (three months). $27 \div 3 = 9$.

Our answer (9) is the average monthly sales for the past 3 months and is an accurate estimation of what we can expect mobile phone sales to be in April. This is the basis of our future orientated report.

As well as speculative sales reports future orientated reports should also consist of expected and possible unforeseen risks and opportunities. Tools and processes that entrap others should be rejected, these processes may seem full of potential but the backlash from using such unethical methods is surely not worth the possible rewards.

Become a Translator

When we tell a story, joke, or even just have a general chat, we have the opportunity to connect directly with our listener's thought patterns and emotions as well as a wealth of other informative facts about them, their lives, likes and dislikes, motives, values, intentions and so on. When communicating with others metaphor and suggestion are arguably two of our most powerful allies and when combined with the proper use of words, we are able to masterfully interact with and conduct those around us. Develop a 'set menu' or 'toolbox' of stories that enable you to cleverly get your point across or instil in others the importance of your values. The best storytellers speak directly to the audience's subconscious, evoking powerful emotions rooted in our most powerful and basic motives and instincts.

It is painfully obvious to most of us that being a boss, manager, leader, coach or pretty much any figure of authority has little, if anything at all to do with their expertise, knowledge or skillset. CEOs and Managing directors commonly require a number of experts on hand to properly analyse patterns, forecasts, and results. This means that inevitably, experts and specialists become integral in the decision-making process. Those with specialised skillsets have the ability to discern meaning from current events which others will have missed or labelled as worthless to effectively predict future events and trends. In our case successfully translating means properly translating the words and actions of others in order to glean information which we can use to our advantage. The basis of this is learning to better understand others (which has been a common theme throughout the book). Translating others allows us to understand and quickly sum up their ideas, values, and obstacles in simple yet appealing ways. We are drawn to those who speak our language, so it is important that we properly translate others so that we can understand them and speak to them on their level. This makes a huge difference when attempting to convey and pass on important information in a way that our audience will understand.

- Pay attention to the words of others, or more correctly, pay attention to the types of words others choose to use. As previously discussed, we all process information in slightly different ways. The best way to identify a person's processing style is by assessing their language by way of the 5 senses.
- Visual thinkers use words and phrases like; see, saw, peripheral, visualise, I see what you mean, I can't see that happening, I saw that one coming, we're in the dark here, there's a light at the end

of the tunnel, perspective, outlook, illustrates, well drawn out, I can picture it now.

- Auditory thinkers use words and phrases like; I hear what you are saying, this opinion is echoed by the group, I like the sound of that, the tone of the message was off, sounding board.

- Kinaesthetic thinkers use words and phrases like; hang in there, get a grip, it is within reach, that idea gives me the creeps, stability, a weighty subject, carries momentum, cold as ice, grasp the situation, the cold light of day, heated debate.

- Once we have noticed a cluster of these words and sayings, we can adopt the same type of language for the remainder of the interaction and all following interactions. This will allow us to 'speak the same language' on an internal level, leading to more meaningful connections with greater rapport and enhanced influence.

Key emotions to watch out for are- ACCEPTANCE, REJECTION, LIKING, DISLIKING, INTEREST, BOREDOM, TRUTH, and DECEPTION.

And Finally, Don't Forget to Smile

A smile conveys friendliness and confidence, there's no need to be fake, people can naturally sense fakes and are untrusting of fake smiles. Smiling is most powerful when matched with the correct, straight, head up posture.

- Smile as you enter the room.
- When meeting new people (remember eye contact).
- Whilst speaking on the phone.
- Throughout a presentation or speaking in public, unless context commands otherwise.

Putting It All Together

All the skills, methods, and techniques covered in this book are twofold in nature. We can use them towards the embitterment of ourselves and the way in which we communicate with others, but we can also use them to effectively read, understand, influence, and covertly manipulate others. We use the information gained from reading others to inform us of our next move, we then adapt our methods accordingly. This will include manipulating and controlling our own emotions and subliminal body language which creates a non-stop loop of reading and adapting ourselves with each circuit bringing us closer to our goal. Each sigh, or smile, wince or grimace, movement of the hand or foot, shift of body weight, what we look at, when we choose not to look, each nod of the head, slip of the tongue, a shaking leg or any other of the plethora of non-verbal communication we inadvertently telegraph all either add up to strengthen or diminish the overall credibility of ourselves and our message. If the impact or believability or our message is compromised then all influence will be lost and we may even damage our chances of influencing any future actions or decisions. In order to achieve our goals, we must be clear about our outcomes and have a vision.

Your vision is generally a clear picture of where you want to be, but the path to making this vision a reality is littered with smaller goals and challenges to overcome. Each goal should represent a benchmark along your path and these goals should each be broken down into manageable objectives that can be completed within a deadline.

To have a vision may sound a little philosophical but in essence, when communicating your ideas to others your vision only requires two aspects. When presenting your vision in a professional environment, it should be handled similarly to a sales pitch, however, in this case, the audience is made of superiors and/or teammates and what you want them to buy is your idea and not products or services. Your vision must motivate you and it must also have the ability to inspire others into action. As your vision is described it will create an image of the future, a future that's better for everyone and we will all make it there together by following your leadership.

As well as the two main aspects mentioned above, when communicating your vision to others you'll want it to include answers to the following:

- What will you/your team achieve?
- Does the vision have congruent values?
- How will it affect you/your team in the long-term?
- How long will it take to accomplish? What are the deadlines, if any?
- What do you need to achieve your vision?
- Exactly what will it take to succeed?
- How will success be measured?
- Will this success cause anyone else's failure?

- Does this vision contain any solid long-term or short-term solutions?

Basic Outcome Clarification Process

Situations change in an instant, they can vary from mildly predictable to wildly out of control and so no fixed set of rules can be applied to all circumstances or every interaction. What is essential is the feasibility of the desired goal as well as the methods that go towards accomplishing it. To do this we must analyse our plans by putting them through an effective clarification process that precisely determines the costs, benefits, obligations (if any) and any overall gains that will be made from following the proposed course of action. Once the overall feasibility of an initiative, project, or task has been decided, there are some fundamental factors that need to be considered before we take action, they are as follows.

How Will the Outcome Affect Those Around Me?

Be ethical, no one wants to have a negative effect on those around them. In most cases, you will find that what's best for the team is also best for the individual. I would strongly advise against sacrificing others for anything other than saving the business or team as a whole. Never risk the safety and wellbeing of others for financial gain. Aim towards creating inclusive projects and systems instead of primarily extractive ones as extractive processes cannot continue long-term and so the overall results will not only detrimental to those being extracted from but also to the power base and long-term influence of the extractor.

Will the Outcome be an Asset, Expense or Liability?

This key question is one that ensures that the vast majority of ideas never get past the drawing board. This is in no way a book containing financial guidance, but with that being taken into account it is wise to classify any potential initiative by its desired outcomes and catalogue it as one of the following:

- An **asset** can be defined as a holding that will provide for you 'long-term' usually either monthly or annually but they can regularly pay out at much less frequent intervals. These assets, which add to your cash flow on a regular/semi-regular basis or which boost the worth of another personal asset are true assets to be held on to for as long as possible. The term asset here also goes further to include anything that proves itself as to continually add strength to or improve team moral as all of these things act to further advance the effectiveness of a business.

- An **expense** can be anything from day to day living costs to unexpected yet crucial running costs such as maintenance, and one-off payments. Carefully consider all of your expenses, in turn, to ensure that hidden among them are not any liabilities disguised as essential expenditures. When you are certain that a particular cost can be classified as an expense, you must then take some time to scrutinize its worth. Could the money spent on this expense be put to better use within my assets without it having a detrimental effect on my quality of life or ability to meet my obligations.

- **Liabilities** should be avoided wherever possible. Generally, they have a regular cost but they may have a daily, weekly, monthly or even annual cost that serves little to no return whatsoever. One of the most common mistakes that people make is in classing their car as an asset when the truth for a lot of drivers out there is that their car is obviously a liability and a burden which causes them to live beyond their means. The extreme example of this is car finance which guarantees a steady stream of cash will be leaving your bank account every month for the foreseeable future, regardless of what happens to the newly purchased car.

Benefits and Costs

When assessing the benefits of an outcome we must again utilise our acuity. The proper assessment of benefits vs costs will involve a number of factors that all affect each other. These are not things to be discussed with other people as the costs, actions, and influence attained through deception and persuasion are our own and inviting others to opine will only convolute and distort our strategies and values.

Obligatory Costs

Here are three basic cost classes that will help you to define whether a particular course of action or financial cost is worthwhile or at least justifiable:

- **Short term costs vs short term benefits**. This is what we experience day in, day out. These include our general living costs as well as the energy we expend being polite and understanding towards the emotions and personal requirements of those around us.

- **Long term costs vs long term benefits** can be very beneficial depending on the obligation and the overall amount and also if the cost is not too regular an outgoing. Although, in most cases, costs that fall into this class frequently turn out to be liabilities. They are rare, exceptions to the above do exist and if shown to be assets can prove to be unquestionably valuable.

- **Short term costs vs long term benefits**, when dealing in matters of persuasion and influence, a short-term cost in exchange for long term benefits is ideal, providing the short-term costs is small and the long-term benefits are guaranteed.

- **Long term costs for short term benefits** should not even be considered unless the cost is minimal and the benefits astronomical, which is extremely rare. Costs in this category should in the vast majority of cases be avoided like the plague.

Be Smarterr

Make a mental note of the acronym, **SMARTERR** that can help us remember the fundamentals of outcome clarification. Is your outcome **Specific, Measurable, Attainable** and **Rational** with a **Timescale**? Once an outcome is reached it must be **Evaluated** and **Refined** and finally, its success should be **Repeated**.

Opportunities for Influence and Persuasion

Psychology, as we know by now plays a huge part in the theories of influence and manipulation. And we have also referenced the mainstream media, marketing, and social media and the ways in which they attempt to influence our thoughts and actions. These influencers can appear almost anywhere and come in almost every form imaginable. This leads to the conclusion that at any given moment is another opportunity to influence others. This includes everything from tweets and social media posts to face to face conversations, social interactions, business meetings, and email sign-offs. Anywhere where we can place visuals or leave a written or electronic message is an opportunity to persuade and convert others to our cause. However, the following examples are those in which employing influential and persuasive are an absolute must:

- Job interviews
- First dates
- Service or product descriptions
- Tenders
- General negotiations (service providers, salespeople, suppliers. authorities, family members, children, etc)
- Collaborations of all kinds
- Use telephone calls to practice vocal skills like tonality, diction, pauses, pace, and persuasive language
- Social media posts

A Final Thought on Personal Development

The most charismatic, influential, and therefore effective communicators, people managers, and leaders are on a constant path of self-development and discovery, the skills from which are then used to succeed in the outside world. Once mastered, they turn the same skills towards more efficiently directing and developing those around them. The cornerstone of self-development is to recognise your own thoughts and actions as well as the consequences involved. Over time you will begin to notice your behavioural patterns, at which point you can begin to modify and change them. The first thing to remember is:

- **Your thoughts become words.**

- **Your words determine your actions.**

- **Your actions become your habits.**

- *Your habits determine your character.*

Your thoughts are not your beliefs and the same goes for other people. They only reflect beliefs and rarely are they entirely accurate, if at all. The main thing to remember about beliefs is that they work in one of two ways, they either enable you, or they limit you. Pay close attention to your beliefs and the impact they have on your day to day life, take a mental note whether the belief is limiting one or whether it is one that enables your success.

Afterword

Congratulations, you made it, I truly hope you enjoyed reading **Psychological Manipulation: Analyzing People, Situations and How to Influence Others Through Covert Persuasion**, and leaned a few things along the way. This is the first book in the **Secrets of The Dark Arts** series, a series that has been designed to streamline and make assessible techniques that are usually overly complicated and unfeasible in the real world. By reading the series you will learn how to prime individuals for more preferable outcomes, master the art of body language and charisma building, influence others through the use of creative Eriksonian language and much more. The series of books focus on the arts of persuasion and manipulation in all their forms and how to use them to effectively embetter the lives of not only yourself but everyone around you. By learning how to read and guide others we take greater responsibility for our choices and the world in which we live, we strengthen our ability to manifest a destiny of our choosing and that, more than anything else, is true freedom.

"May your influence encompass all"